SATHER CLASSICAL LECTURES

VOLUME TWELVE

1936

ROMAN SATIRE:
ITS OUTLOOK ON SOCIAL LIFE

ROMAN SATIRE

Its Outlook on Social Life

BY

J. WIGHT DUFF, D. LITT., LL. D.

EMERITUS PROFESSOR OF CLASSICS,
ARMSTRONG COLLEGE, NEWCASTLE-UPON-TYNE,
IN THE UNIVERSITY OF DURHAM

FELLOW OF THE BRITISH ACADEMY
HONORARY FELLOW OF PEMBROKE COLLEGE, OXFORD

UNIVERSITY OF CALIFORNIA PRESS
BERKELEY, CALIFORNIA
1936

UNIVERSITY OF CALIFORNIA PRESS
BERKELEY, CALIFORNIA

CAMBRIDGE UNIVERSITY PRESS
LONDON, ENGLAND

PA
6095
D8

PRINTED IN THE UNITED STATES OF AMERICA

VNIVERSITATI CALIFORNIENSI
AD AVREAM ILLAM IANVAM OCCIDENTIS SOLIS SPECTANTI
IPSIQVE LVMEN DOCTRINAE LATE DIFFVNDENTI
HASCE PRAELECTIONES

IOANNES WIGHT DVFF

ADVENA BRITANNVS BENIGNE EXCEPTVS
GRATISSIMO ANIMO
DEDICAT

CONTENTS

PREFACE

THIS CONTRIBUTION to the history of Roman satire represents in its eight chapters, with only slight alterations and additions, the lectures which I delivered at Berkeley in the Spring Semester of 1936 as Sather Professor of Classical Literature in the University of California.

The notes, which follow the text, indicate the chief ancient sources drawn upon and the chief modern authorities on the subject. Most of the illustrative translations were written specially for my course; but, in addition to many thus published for the first time, I have pleasure in acknowledging the kind permission given me by Messrs. Ernest Benn to quote a few of my own verse renderings from Seneca, Phaedrus, Persius, and Juvenal, as contained in *A Literary History of Rome in the Silver Age*.

I am deeply grateful to my wife for typing my manuscript and for giving valuable help in proofreading.

J. WIGHT DUFF

BERKELEY, CALIFORNIA,
June 17, 1936.

CHAPTER I

SATIRE ANCIENT AND MODERN

Satura quidem tota nostra est
QUINTILIAN *Inst. Or.* X. i. 93

BEFORE a survey of Roman satire limited to a course of eight lectures is entered upon, there are on the threshold, as it were, certain confronting problems which, if they cannot be fully discussed, must at least be stated. Among those preliminary questions, *adverso in limine*, there is the general and fundamental one, What is Satire? What does it connote as a literary genre? What is its function in the hands of English as well as Latin satirists? How is satire distributed among different forms of literature? And then there are a few special questions: What did the Latin word *satura* mean? Was there a dramatic *satura*? Was satire the peculiar possession of the Roman genius, as Quintilian declared? If so, what was meant by his claim? Was there a Greek satire?

Modern analogies are sometimes helpful in throwing light upon problems in ancient literature and history. The subject of Roman satire, even with respect to definition, presents initial difficulties which may be illustrated by parallels in current English. I take two statements which might be made today, both with truth, and yet apparently in conflict the one with the other. We may say, on the one hand, "Satire is seldom[1]* written now, or at any rate enjoys a small vogue," and, on the other hand, "Satire is a constantly recurring feature in much of our contemporary literature." It is obvious that "satire" is being used with different meanings in these two sentences. The first means that we do not often now find satire published in the traditional English couplet as handled by Dryden in *Absalom and Achitophel* and *The Medal*, by Pope in *The Rape of the Lock* and the *Dunciad*, and by Byron, at least in his *English Bards and*

---

* Superior figures refer to notes, pp. 169–184.

Scotch Reviewers, *The Waltz*, *The Curse of Minerva*, and *The Age of Bronze*. There is significance in the fact that Byron himself in his satiric work departed from the couplet into the octet, based on Pulci's *Morgante Maggiore*, which is familiar to us in *The Vision of Judgement* (a lampoon rather than a satire) and in *Don Juan*. But, whatever the meter, whether old Skelton's short lines, or the octosyllabics of *Hudibras*, or the couplets of the classical English satirists, or the later Byronic stanza, the truth emerges that few authors now compose separate poems to be entitled satires as authors did during the heyday of the genre in the seventeenth and eighteenth centuries, the period when the influence of Latin satire was at its strongest on English literature. The Romantic Movement contributed to oust the conventional form. But to return to the second statement, that "satire is a constantly recurring feature in much of our contemporary literature," this means, and it is also true, that though formal and conventional satire has waned, the spirit of satire has not died. Satire in the sense of the satiric spirit survives vigorously, notably in the novel and the drama. We must then carefully distinguish between "satire" meaning formal satire, and "satire" meaning "the satiric." This distinction we shall find to be of importance when we have later to contrast, in the matter of satire, Greek and Latin literature; and this leads to definition of satire and examination of its function.

One cannot do better here than begin with a definition valuable in that it belongs to the period when satires as separate productions were still a living form of literature in England. This is Dr. Johnson's definition of satire: "a poem in which wickedness or folly is censured." There are two points to observe at once. First, this definition places English satire in a direct line of descent from Latin satire, because it assigns to it a meaning consonant with that which Lucilius attached to it and which was taken over, with modifications, by Horace and later by Juvenal. Secondly, Johnson recognized the word "satire" as originally a Latin word: he derived it from "*satira*," anciently "*satura*," and expressly stated that it was not from the Greek word σάτυρος for a Satyr. The supposed connection with the Satyrs of Greek mythology, countenanced by ancient grammarians, but exploded by Casaubon's famous essay of 1605,[2] led in the past to a good deal of confused thinking and fanciful speculation: it died all the more slowly in England because the old spelling of "satire" was "satyr"—Dryden's form, in fact, spelt and pronounced indistinguishably from the English form of the Greek word with which it has no kindred. It is noteworthy that the derivative adjectives "satiric" from "satire," and "Satyric" from "Satyr" still sound exactly alike to the ear. This confusion led in the sixteenth and seventeenth centuries to the curious notion that the half-bestial woodland demons, the Satyrs, were endowed with a gift of censoriousness. The Oxford *New English Dictionary* gives as its definition of "satire": "in early use a discursive composition in verse treating of a variety of subjects; in classical use a poem in which prevalent follies or vices are assailed with ridicule or with serious denunciation." It proceeds to explain that this is a specific application of Latin *satura* in the sense of a medley, a point to be glanced at later. But an extension of meaning is sanctioned by general usage, the ultimate arbiter of correctness, as Horace acknowledged in the *Ars Poetica*, and it is therefore pointed out that satire has been used from the seventeenth century in its wider sense to include the employment in speaking as well as in writing "of sarcasm, irony, ridicule, etc. in denouncing, exposing or deriding vice, folly, abuses or evils of every kind."

Here we have passed away from the poetic form which normally followed Latin example and have reached the broader connotation in which, as we shall see, the claim is made that "satire" exists under various forms in Greek literature. Satire, indeed, when it means the satiric spirit, occurs in all literature, including the Bible; for it is well exemplified in Elijah's ironic advice to the prophets of Baal: "and it came to pass at noon that Elijah mocked them and said, 'Cry aloud; for he is a god: either he is talking or he is pursuing or he is in a journey, or peradventure he sleepeth and must be awaked'" (I Kings, xviii. 27). This satire of sarcastic counsel is common in repartee and in formal oratory; for example, when Cicero (*De Provinciis Consularibus*, 12), who wants Gabinius recalled from Syria, says, "Keep for a longer period in the province a man who makes covenants with the enemy respecting the allies" (*Retinete igitur in provincia diutius eum . . .*). In formal satire a good illustration is Juvenal's apostrophe to Hannibal as a type of the ambitious warrior:

> Go! o'er the cruel Alps career, you fool,
> To charm young essayists in the rhetoric school.

> *i, demens et saevas curre per Alpes*
> *ut placeas pueris et declamatio fias.*
>
> (Juv. X. 166-167)

Satire in the broader sense pervades English prose works of the eighteenth century like Defoe's ironical and misunderstood *Shortest Way with the Dissenters*, or Swift's *Tale of a Tub*, or his *Gulliver's Travels*, charged with his bitterest disgust for humanity, or French works of the same century like Voltaire's *Babouc* and *Candide*. Addison and Steele in a more genial Horatian spirit used their contributions to the *Spectator* to chastise without malice human weaknesses, so that the essay also became a vehicle for the satiric. With this wide expansion of the old Roman conception we can go beyond Voltaire's mordant wit and recognize satire in the lifelike pictures which Fielding's novels present of the manners and morals of Georgian England and in Hogarth's contemporary paintings and engravings, equally realistic in their different medium of art. It is to be found not only in the tirades of a Thomas Carlyle, but also in the fictitious country of Samuel

Butler's *Erewhon*, as readers once found it in Lilliput; for to draw any ideal is to some extent an implicit satire on the real and, if this be kept in view, there is satire in Plato's *Republic* and still more in the extravaganza of Aristophanes' *Birds*. But this satiric attitude to life may also be expressed in forms of no very sustained length. In the Greek Anthology and in Martial an epigram will serve the purpose in quatrain or couplet—the briefest form of all, unless we include certain proverbial sayings pregnant with criticism on human conduct, such as "There's no fool like an old fool," or "Acquittal of the guilty damns the judge," *Iudex damnatur cum nocens absolvitur*, the motto which *The Edinburgh Review* took from Publilius Syrus to mark its severity in criticism. So too the cynical apophthegm by the same Publilius, quite in keeping with Juvenal's Sixth Satire, "A woman is good at last when she's openly bad," *Aperte mala cum est mulier, tum demum est bona*, or yet again some of the hexametric *monosticha* which have come down among the *Dicta Catonis*, such as "Calm looks do sometimes cloak a loathsome mind," *Nonnumquam vultu tegitur mens taetra sereno*.

Satire, just as it played a part in Greek and Latin comedy, colors a long line of plays, whether in a spirit of easygoing gaiety like Farquhar's *Beaux' Stratagem* of 1707, or such light operas as Gilbert and Sullivan's *Patience*, which ridiculed the Victorian aesthetic movement, or more recently even in serious plays like Galsworthy's *Strife* or *The Silver Box*. Farquhar's play is significant because his prologue proclaims drama as one of the vehicles of satire:

> When strife disturbs or sloth corrupts an age,
> Keen satire is the business of the stage,

and elsewhere, in his miscellany *Love and Business*, he introduced into a discourse on comedy a definition which would equally suit the amiable type of satire represented by Horace: "Comedy," according to Farquhar, "is no more at present

than a well framed tale handsomely told as an agreeable vehicle for counsel or reproof." On these lines his own dramas
ought to have been entitled to wear without a blush the motto
castigat ridendo mores (chastening manners through ridicule),
but his lively concourse of military officers and flippant beaux
admits of little pause for the "counsel or reproof" advocated
in his definition. I have adduced his attitude not as anything new (for it agrees with the ancient description of comedy
as a *speculum vitae*), but as a reminder of the function performed by Aristophanes' more polemic plays in Athens and
of Horace's pronouncement that the Roman satirist Lucilius
depended entirely on the outspoken old Greek comedy.

There must, indeed, always be a kinship between satire
and comedy. They are linked on the ground of social outlook: they are alike dependent for success on that power of
observation which creates and guarantees their realism. Nothing in Latin literature is more typically Roman than the social outlook in its satire. Except perhaps in the letters of
Cicero and of the younger Pliny and, to a less extent, in those
of Seneca, nowhere else is the social outlook so clear, and the
notion so regularly conveyed that the proper study of mankind is man. In satire, however, the social interest is coupled
with a didactic aim which Cicero does not introduce into his
letters, though it powerfully permeates the *Epistulae Mo-
rales* of Seneca. What gives satire its vital importance in Latin
literature is not poetic charm, for, though in verse, it is not
poetry of the highest order: it is rather its faithful representation of contemporary life and its comments thereupon.
Roman satire stands out the more prominently in this respect because Latin comedies based upon contemporary life,
the *fabulae togatae* and *fabulae tabernariae*, have all perished,
leaving behind only titles and occasional fragments. We have
suffered thus through the unkindness of devouring time the
loss of one most interesting section of Latin literature, where
realism predominated. This gap the satirists have to fill for

us: and for their valuable witness to social life we are indebted to that gift of observation which is one of the secrets of the appeal made by satire, as it is a secret of the appeal made by several other literary arts—that of the novelist, for instance.

No more appropriate example in this field can be adduced than Balzac, whose fiction so greatly rested on meticulous attention to detail and was explicitly designed to constitute a huge *Comédie humaine*. He could be grim enough in the Juvenalian realism of scenes of calculating wickedness and gloomy pathos, but his light touches in comic vein have also the verisimilitude which makes the reader see his characters. I cannot refrain from citing Pierre Grassou as an instance in point. Pierre, a mediocrity among painters, has become a favorite with the *bourgeoisie*, and Balzac is highly entertaining about the middle-class family that engages Pierre to paint their portraits—the corpulent father with a head like nothing so much as a melon surmounting a pumpkin which moves on two roots improperly called legs; his wife resembling a coconut with a head of mahogany and feathers of a first-class hearse floating over her bonnet; and his daughter, a young asparagus in green and yellow with carroty hair "which," says Balzac, "a Roman would have adored." This is more than an ordinary onlooker would have seen; by exaggerating a few peculiarities it approaches caricature; but the artist's eye has picked out resemblances which present the figures vividly before us, as Horace and Juvenal can do.

A similarly characteristic keenness of observation explains in some degree the strength and success of the older English schools of portraiture and painting. How does it operate in satire? Observation and fidelity to what is observed, not only externally, but also psychologically in the deeper realm of character, constitute a realistic check upon unlicensed imagination: they guarantee a certain self-control and restraint which appear admirably represented in Horace. Even in Juvenal the necessity of respecting truth of observation acts as a rein upon hyperbole: and, though he delights in exaggeration, he trusts his intelligent reader to make from what sounds excessive the deduction necessary to relate the overstatements to actual life. No one believes his suggestion that the noisy spouter of *recitationes* cracked the columns in a garden; but it is a fair point whereby to convey forcibly one at least of the drawbacks of these unending literary *séances*. Satire, then, can never exist successfully far apart from real things and real character. This truth underlies Swift's definition in his preface to *The Battle of the Books:* "Satire is a sort of glass wherein beholders do generally discover everybody's face but their own." True to his manner, he has added a little mischievous spice; but it is doubtful whether this is not justifiable in fact. So much has traditionally been taught about the reformative aim of the satirist that there is something salutary in the ironic reminder that readers of satire are readier to see other people's faults than to recognize their own. Horace goes straight to the point in his *de te fabula narratur:* "Thou art the man." Under this aspect satire is a literary medicine for a world morally and socially out of health; and, if this holds good, the satirist is a kind of doctor. The more diseased the world, the more unpleasant are the home truths which the physician may have to reveal while he points the way back to better things. Holding the mirror up to human failings, the satirist cannot avoid being implicitly a preacher; for though he reflects follies, wrongs, or vice, it detracts from the moral effect if he seem to revel in them. His very attack argues some belief in progress: it would be pointless otherwise: he would fain purge, blister, cauterize, even amputate, if so he might make a cure. The question then arises, Can a writer of satire be consistently pessimistic? He should have faith enough to think he can do good by denouncing evil: otherwise his labor is thrown away and doubt cast upon his motives. This is a consideration to be kept in mind for its bearing on the pessimism which is ascribed to Juvenal.

The function of satire is not merely to sting and amuse alternately. Something constructive and instructive must underlie the social criticism involved in Horace's laugh or Juvenal's malice. Horace, as sympathetic readers know, has a philosophy of life to convey; and it is suggestive that Juvenal, in that famous satire of his which has exhibited in their nakedness the vanity of so many human desires, pulled himself up to inquire whether there is left to mankind nothing to wish for, nothing to pray for. There follows, in Stoic vein, lines of advice which the satirist, in spite of one flippant verse which he could not resist the temptation to insert, feels will secure happiness for the individual and health for a community. His doctrine is to trust the gods and do the right. The humor manifest in Horace accompanies a deep seriousness. This union is the idea conveyed in the Greek term τὸ σπουδαιογέλοιον or σπουδογέλοιον. Behind what is queer or ludicrous or reprehensible in human society there is the element of suffering and sorrow: besides the pettiness there is also the nobility of human life which must at times disarm the satirist and soften his attacks by awakening sympathy and a sense of pity. Horace shows this understanding spirit toward human failings. He knows that he has his own faults, takes himself to task, and is therefore charitable toward the faults of other men. And Juvenal, so often savage in his indictments, has finely argued[3] that Nature's gift of tears to mankind means that she has given us tender hearts, that man's inhumanity to man is a violation of Nature, and that it is an inborn impulse to be troubled at a friend's danger or moved by the death of some girl or by the committal to earth of a baby too little for a funeral pyre. For the moment Juvenal seems to strike a note in harmony with Virgil's famous *Sunt lacrimae rerum et mentem mortalia tangunt,* "Tears haunt the world: man's fortunes touch the heart."

So much in brief for the main function and motives of satire. Its themes, its materials are as wide as humanity, *quicquid agunt homines,* in Juvenal's words. It possesses therefore an infinite variety of subject which must win interest for it; and this interest is enhanced by the variety of its method. So far as a satiric element appeared under different forms in Greek literature, it was in large part a mixture of ridicule and didacticism (τὸ σπουδαιογέλοιον). In Latin literature satire was much more specially developed. It attained a separate form with the hexameter as the classic meter for its greatest exponents, Lucilius, Horace, Persius, and Juvenal. There was also the blend of verse with prose in the Menippean satire of Varro, Petronius, and Seneca. To convey its pictures and its lessons, those who practiced satire employed in different degrees, according to temperament or theme, such means as sharp invective, ridicule fierce or gentle, coarseness, irony, burlesque and parody, dialogue, narrative (including personal adventure and other autobiographic elements), fable, homily, literary criticism—a variety, indeed, which preserves the Latin medley from becoming stereotyped or hackneyed, and in the hands of great artists, like Horace and Juvenal, explains the powerful influence which Roman satire has wielded in the world.

Yet for verse satire it cannot be asserted that its place is with the highest in the hierarchy of poetry. Horace, in many ways its greatest representative, labors under no illusion regarding its literary assessment. His own satires he expressly ranked below the poetry of his odes: their very words, because of their subject, were nearer to ordinary talk, *sermoni propiora.* But, this being so, satire is also unquestionably closer to the workaday concerns of human society; and no division of poetry seems, therefore, in the view of the plain reader, more obviously to illustrate Matthew Arnold's definition of poetry as "a criticism of life."

Contemporary satire, largely represented by novels and plays rather than by poetry, exhibits one striking difference from the satire of the ancients. There is less confidence on the part of the modern satirist that he himself stands on sure ground in his social criticism. He would perhaps go the length of subscribing to the Stoic doctrine, though not for Stoic reasons, that all the world is mad; he might admit that much in the civilization of today spells insanity; but he might equally feel distrust of his own complete sanity. This loss of sureness seems to characterize the present-day attitude in contrast with that of even a few generations ago, in contrast with Dickens, for example; and it serves to explain why many novels and plays now appear, after a series of negations, to end on a merely interrogative note. Clear it may be what the author dislikes: it is not so clear what principles he upholds or what remedies he has to suggest. The ancient satirist had a less complex world to survey, so that it is easier under his criticisms to grasp his positive beliefs and to understand his outlook. Here, then, Roman satire has something simpler and more definite to offer as a subject of study.

In these introductory remarks upon certain aspects of satire repeated reference has been made to English literature; but I feel, if this needs apology, that the modern instances are eminently justifiable and instructive in the approach to a study of Roman satire—first, because the work of a brilliant and varied galaxy of satirists has been one of the great achievements of English letters, just as satire was one of the great achievements of Latin literature; secondly, because not only is "satire" originally a Latin word, but the attitude of the typical English satirists was inherited, indeed in large part copied, from Rome. The Lucilian invective, mitigated and tempered by Horace, and in great measure resuscitated by Juvenal, was the inspiring exemplar. The lines by Dryden and Pope which rise most readily to the memory from the great period of English satire are marked by a Latin concision and often by a scathing Juvenalian ring: for instance—

To that unfeather'd two-legg'd thing—a son,
(Dryden, *Absalom and Achitophel*)

half suggesting the younger Pliny's *omnium bipedum nequissimus;* or

> The rest to some faint meaning make pretence,
> But Shadwell never deviates into sense;
>
> (Dryden, *MacFlecknoe*)

or

> But in the course of one revolving moon
> Was chymist, fiddler, statesman and buffoon;
>
> (Dryden, *Absalom and Achitophel*)

> Damn with faint praise, assent with civil leer,
> And without sneering, teach the rest to sneer,
> Willing to wound and yet afraid to strike,
> Just hint a fault and hesitate dislike;
>
> (Pope, *To Dr. Arbuthnot*)

or, with the additional note of didacticism on literary subjects familiar in ancient satire, the lines which open Pope's *Essay on Criticism*,

> 'Tis hard to say if greater want of skill
> Appears in writing or in judging ill,

or the constantly quoted

> A little learning is a dangerous thing:
> Drink deep or taste not the Pierian spring.
>
> (Pope, *Essay on Criticism*)

Further, it is important to show clearly that we now use the term "satire" in a much wider sense than the Romans did. We apply it freely and without qualification to what may be called incidental satire—that is, passages, short or long, of a satiric nature interspersed in literature which is not formally satire at all. Latin literature, like all other literatures, has abundance of such incidental satire. It occurs in drama; for instance, the caricature of Euclio's stinginess in the *Aulularia* of Plautus (*Aul.* 300 sqq.), "He wouldn't present you even with hunger, if you asked for it: he treasures the parings of his nails"; and comedy can furnish scores of other examples. It occurs often in oratory; for instance, Cicero's mock-serious banter of Cato's Stoic rigidity in the *Pro Murena*, or the violent onslaughts of the *In Pisonem*, or many ironic touches with *credo, nimirum, egregius*. It occurs in the arguments of the elder Seneca's *Controversiae;* for example, I. vi. 1, of the pirate's daughter married to a young Roman whom she had freed from her father's custody, "a most promising wife," says the heavy Roman *paterfamilias*, "a most promising daughter-in-law, who is capable of loving even a prisoner and hating even her father." It occurs also in the sarcastic humor of the younger Seneca's essay-like *Letters;* for example, i. 3, "Nobody thinks he owes anything for taking your time"; xxxvi. 4, the picture of an "elementarius senex," a grammar-school old fellow learning what he ought to have studied long ago; or lxxxvi. 7, on villas with gorgeous mosaic pavements, "We've grown so fine that we won't have anything but precious stones in our flooring to tread upon!"

The point is that in none of these would a Roman have applied the word *satura* as a generic term: special words like *irrisio, illusio, vituperatio, insectatio, acerbitas, dissimulatio* (corresponding to the Greek εἰρωνεία[4]), *cavillatio, facetiae, sales* or Horace's *sal niger*, would be required to suit different passages. *Invectiva*, neuter plural, is a late usage, in Ammianus, but the verb *invehi* is frequent and classical for verbal attack. Horace's word *sermo*, a chat or *causerie*, is not applicable to satire in general.

Over fifty years ago, Professor Nettleship of Oxford began his essay on "The Original Form of the Roman Satura"[5] by remarking on the trouble which the name *satura* had given to scholars. Since his day a vast amount of attention has been given to the word, its original and its developed meanings, its use as a title, and its application in Livy to a form of drama. It would be inappropriate in a limited course on Ro-

man Satire to attempt to follow the discussions on this difficult subject. Only its fringe, therefore, can be touched here.
The ancients themselves were puzzled by the word *satura*:
the moderns have not reached complete agreement on the
problems involved.[6] The grammarian Diomedes,[7] who is later
than the fourth-century grammarians Donatus and Chari-
sius, offers a choice among four explanations: (1) from the
σάτυροι (*a Satyris*), an idea now discountenanced; (2) from
a full platter of various fruit offerings called *satura*, illustrated by the phrase *satura lanx*;[8] (3) from a kind of food
stuffing (*farcimen*) for which Varro's authority is cited twice;
(4) from a law of what we may call an "omnibus" character,
illustrated by the phrase *per saturam*, which, however, implies logically the preëxistence of the noun *satura*. Under-
neath the second, third, and fourth of these explanations
there lies a common notion of mixture or medley, and this is
indicated in a straightforward manner by the synonym *farcimen*, explained, says Diomedes, by Varro as a stuffing of
many ingredients (*multis rebus refertum*), and backed by a
definite recipe quoted from the second book of Varro's *Plautine Questions* for a compote of raisins and pearl barley with
a dash of mead and pine kernels, which we may fancy gave
a flavor like that in the resinato wine of modern Greece: and
the mixture is concluded with the words, "and some add
pomegranate seeds."

This prevailing sense of mixture may be reasonably taken
as the original sense: it is not difficult to transfer it to that
sense of a literary medley which was never wholly disso-
ciated from the term *satura*, as Juvenal's "hotchpotch of my
booklet" (*nostri farrago libelli*) shows at the beginning of the
second century A.D. If the dramatic *satura* recorded by Livy
is accepted as historical, it is not difficult in that use of the
word also to see the appropriateness of the extension of what
was originally a culinary term to a semiliterary production.[9]
Among parallel usages may be mentioned "farce" from the

Italian *farsa*, stuffing; "olio" applied in a literary sense; and "Rag-pie" as a students' magazine.

The earliest occurrence of the word *satura* in an extant literary text is in the first line of Horace's second book of *sermones* issued in 30 B.C., where he says, "There are some people who think me too cutting in satire," *sunt quibus in satura videor nimis acer.* The word occurs only twice in Horace; there, at the beginning of the second book, and later in II. vi. 17, where he asks, "On what should I preferably throw light in the satires of my prosaic muse?" *quid prius illustrem saturis musaque pedestri?* Much has been made of the absence of the word in his first book of satires; but it has been pointed out[10] that it was not common Roman practice, either in poetry or in prose, to make frequent use of generic literary terms. Cicero, for instance, though greatly interested in literary criticism and constantly quoting authors in different genres, does not seem to employ such ordinary terms as *epos, elegi, lyricus, palliata.* It has, however, been argued that Horace's postponement of his use of the term *satura* means that only during the decade between 40 and 30 B.C., when readers and critics at Rome felt a revival of interest in Lucilius, did they realize the need for using the word *satura* not simply for a medley, but for the polemic and censorious writings of Lucilius; and one reason suggested for Horace's alleged shyness in adopting the word is that he disliked accepting a term which came from the group of literary enthusiasts with whose intemperate laudation of Lucilius he was too critical to agree. But there is good reason to hold that Lucilius' poems had for sixty or seventy years before been known as *saturae*; and it is hard to believe that grammarians, when they explicitly referred words and phrases to such-and-such a book of the Satires of Ennius or Lucilius, were not quoting original titles but only employing a later interpretative classification. For example, Nonius Marcellus in the fourth century A.D.[11] quotes a line which he specifies as from Ennius' *Satyrae*, Book I; Macrobius records *tristis*, meaning "harsh to the taste," as occurring in the fourth book of Ennius' *Saturae*. Quotations from Lucilius' Books I–XXV are made by Nonius under this sort of formula, "Lucilius in the first book of his satires" (*Lucilius Satyrarum libro primo*). Two centuries earlier, Suetonius[12] mentions Lucilius' compositions as *saturae*; and as for Varro, the list of his many works given in a letter by Jerome records separately his "Books of Satires" (*Satyrarum libri*) and his other kind of satires, the "Menippean" (*Satyrarum Menippearum libri*), which were based on Menippus of Gadara and combined verse with prose. There can be little doubt that Jerome's information goes back ultimately through Suetonius to Varro himself, and little warrant for the suspicion that Varro's own titles had been altered. We have evidence from the second century in Gellius' *Attic Nights*[13] for *Saturae Menippeae* as the title of Varro's work, and no proof to justify Professor Hendrickson's conjecture that poems by Ennius and Lucilius bore some such title as *poemata per saturam* instead of simply *saturae*.

Opinion differs on the question whether, as used by Ennius and Lucilius, the title *saturae* in the plural implied that each book constituted a *satura*, meaning a collection of miscellaneous pieces, or that each individual poem was called a *satura*. In Horace's question quoted above, *quid prius illustrem saturis?*, the word seems most naturally to apply to separate poems, as it apparently also does in its solitary occurrence in the plural in Juvenal at the end of the third satire,[14] where Umbricius promises to come over from the seaside to visit the poet in his rural home: "I'll come with my marching boots on (*caligatus*) to your cool countryside as a listener to your satires (*saturarum auditor*), unless they scorn me." The word occurs three times elsewhere[15] in Juvenal, always in the singular, and always meaning satire in general.

All three occurrences are significant. The first is the fa-

miliar early note struck by Juvenal in his first satire[16]—*difficile est saturam non scribere*, that is, the hard thing is not to
write satire but to refrain from it, when an author looks out
on the social enormities around. Anger, Juvenal's motive
force, is stirred by what he mentions in this context—an inappropriate marriage, a masculine woman a-hunting, the
insufferable airs of an upstart, the parade of wealth got by
dishonesty. No direct assertion is here made that satire is a
reforming agency. There is perhaps slightly more implica-
tion of the sort at IV. 106, where Rubrius, one of Domitian's
guests, is declared to be, in view of his past evil reputation,
"more shameless than a profligate actually writing satire,"
improbior saturam scribente cinaedo. Substantially this is a
case of the pot calling the kettle black, and suggests that
reasonably good character is expected in one who ventures
to turn monitor. The passage is illustrated in the scholia from
one of the bypaths of satire by what Tacitus records[17] of
Afranius Quintianus, a conspirator against Nero. A man of
unclean life, he had been lampooned (*probroso carmine dif-
famatus*) by the Emperor, who, we know, had little reason,
beyond experience, to write upon the subject of immorality.
The remaining instance[18] has a very special literary interest,
because it indicates some degree of consciousness in Juvenal
that his inspiration, which drew its force from fervent wrath,
impelled him to make satire do a work which it had never
done before.[19] The avowal comes toward the close of his long
tirade against women in the sixth satire: "All this merely
our invention, you say (*fingimus haec*)! Satire has borrowed
the high tragic buskin (*altum satura sumente cothurnum*):
we've gone beyond the limit and the law of previous satirists
(*finem egressi legemque priorum*) and we wildly declaim with
loud Sophoclean tones an impressive strain unknown to the
Rutulian hills and the Latin sky"—in other words, it may
be urged perhaps that "I, Juvenal, am too imaginative (*fingimus haec*), too tragic, too much in the grand style, too

Greek, too little in the Latin tradition. Indeed there is something individual, something new in Juvenal which forces one to realize that modern satire would not have the same meaning without him. Persius, in Nero's time, never uses the word *satura* in his verse, though it appears in his title.

Quintilian, the chief professor of rhetoric in the first century, uses *satura* as a generic term for the division of literature so named or for a collection of poems.[20] He opens his special passage about *satura*[21] with his assertion that it is entirely Roman, illustrating it by the names of Lucilius, Horace, and Persius and by remarks on each (Juvenal's satires being as yet unpublished): then, after declaring that there are satirists in his own time whose names would be preserved in the future, he adds the important classification of a second and older sort of *satura* (*alterum illud etiam prius saturae genus*) composed by Terentius Varro and not restricted to a variety of verse-forms, but combining prose as well. The allusion is to the *Menippean Satires*, which must be discussed at a later point.

This sketch of the use of the term *satura* may be concluded instructively by glancing at the two clear occurrences[22] of the word in Martial. They are both in the plural. One is in an epigram (XI.10) on the poet Turnus, who "devoted his mighty intellect to satires" so as to avoid rivaling his brother Memor in writing tragedy; the other is in the author's appeal (XII.94) to Tucca, who has been imitating Martial in every form of composition, to leave him some division of literature to work at without rivalry: "We venture on satires: you toil to be a Lucilius," *audemus saturas: Lucilius esse laboras*. What is noticeable here is the proof that Lucilius, toward the end of the first century, that is, two hundred years after his time, is reckoned, as he was by Juvenal about the same period, to be a typical writer of satire, which is consequently viewed as combative and censorious, in fact the *maledicum carmen* of outspoken attack.

The traditional belief in the existence at Rome of a crude musical farce called *Satura* rests upon a vexed passage in Livy VII. ii which sketches the development of early drama through five stages. The passage is very similar to one in Valerius Maximus, which either paraphrases Livy or draws from the same source as he did: it also uses the term *saturae* for one of the stages at which the dramatic art arrived.[23] Further, there is appreciable resemblance, though not complete parallelism, to the poetic account of the evolution of Latin drama in Horace, *Epistles* II. i. 139-160. The five stages according to Livy were: (1) stately religious dances (*haud indecoros motus*) imported from Etruria in 364 B.C. to appease the gods in time of plague, and performed by Etruscan dancers to flute music without words; (2) burlesques of these dances by young Roman amateurs, who indulged in impromptu jocular dialogue with gestures to match, and by their performances won considerable popularity; (3) *saturae*, performed by native professionals, in which a departure was made from the Fescennine-like jesting of the previous stage, song and gesture being accompanied with flute music; (4) plays introduced by Livius Andronicus with regular plots on Greek models; (5) a revival of the burlesques of the second stage by young Roman amateurs who left the performance of dramas to actors and gave their light performances as after-pieces(*exodia*), generally in association with the Atellan plays.

The passage was regarded by Otto Jahn in 1867[24] as an aetiological account of primitive Roman drama constructed by some scholar—Varro was his guess—from whom Livy had borrowed. This hint was developed some twenty years later by Leo, followed, though not in all details, by Professor Hendrickson, their general line of argument being that Livy was here reproducing some pre-Varronian sketch of Roman drama artificially drawn as a parallel to the Aristotelian account of the development of Greek drama.[25] The *satura* was considered to be an invented feature designed by its insertion to match the old Attic Comedy. Horace's account already mentioned, though it does not introduce the term *satura* and though it does not absolutely agree in detail with Livy's, was equally suspect. But the traditional view has been upheld by several American scholars who have indicated difficulties and inconsistencies in the skeptical position.[26] The arguments for and against cannot be gone into here; but it may be said that, on the whole, the tendency recently has been to accept Livy's account, which introduces the term *satura* in a natural way as a recognized term needing no special explanation beyond the emphatic phrase which refers to the meaning of the word, *impletas modis saturas*. Livy was engaged on his seventh book probably not long before 20 B.C.,[27] about ten years after Horace's second book of *sermones* appeared. There is no ancient record of any direct connection between a dramatic *satura* and literary satire; but the dramatic traits which are universally recognized in Roman satire are to many eyes a testimony to its descent from this haphazard, varied, and plotless type of early farce.[28]

Near the opening of this chapter two sentences were given which appeared to clash in regard to modern satire: toward its close it is appropriate to cite two well-known statements regarding ancient satire which appear to contradict each other. Quintilian, on the one hand, claiming satire for the Romans, remarked, "Satire at any rate is wholly our own."[29] Horace, on the other hand, referring to Lucilius, who gave to Roman satire its distinctive character, says that he entirely depends (*omnis pendet*) upon the Old Greek Comedy.[30] The clash has been much discussed. Both remarks state a truth: both taken without qualification or explanation are incorrect. All Roman satire, though a thoroughly Roman thing, owed a great deal to the Greeks; and Lucilius in particular was indebted to many Greek sources other than the comic drama. The spirit of satire is universal: it belongs to all nations, and the Greeks had used for satiric purposes their gifts of parody and irony, their sharp *iambi*, their mocking comedies, their philosophical dialogues, their ethical discourses. Yet it remains a fact that there existed in Greece no separate form of literature which could be called "satire" in the sense in which we moderns, still using the old Roman term and influenced by Roman usage, can nowadays speak of "the satires of Lucilius," "the satires of Horace," "the satires of Persius," "the satires of Juvenal." The separate genre was a Roman invention, and it went through separate phases in the hands of its four chief exponents. No other literary form in Latin had a career so long and varied from the great days of the republic up to the second century of the empire. A point to stress in relation to Quintilian's pronouncement is that he knew what he was writing about: widely versed in both Greek and Latin, he was an experienced teacher and critic, not unduly biased in favor of the national literature. Just before his *Satura quidem tota nostra est* he has remarked on the challenge which Latin literature could maintain in the field of elegy. Coming to *satura*,[31] he finds that its field belongs entirely to the Roman, in the sense that the Greeks never developed this separate form of literature. They did not compete. This negatives the contention[32] that Quintilian is claiming supremacy for his fellow countrymen: it would be pointless to say that Romans bear off the palm in a contest where there were no other entrants.

As for the remarks on Lucilius by Horace at the opening of the fourth satire of the first book,[33] the passage must be viewed under the aspect of Lucilian satire on which special emphasis is laid. That aspect is the quality of outspokenness (*libertas*) in condemnation of moral delinquents:

> *Si quis erat dignus describi quod malus ac fur,*
> *quod moechus foret aut sicarius aut alioqui*
> *famosus, multa cum libertate notabant.*

This, he says, was the way of Eupolis and Cratinus and Aristophanes as well as other authors of the Old Greek Comedy, and in this sense the Old Comedy is written all over Lucilius; for he followed it in its aggressive spirit, though he changed the meter. The objects of attack here instanced by Horace are offenders against morality, the thief, adulterer, or assassin; but he might fairly have added the keen political outlook in Aristophanic plays, for this field too, in spite of different literary methods and form, exhibited not a little in common between Lucilius and the great comic dramatist of Athens.

CHAPTER II

GREEK PRECURSORS OF ROMAN SATIRE —AND ENNIUS

Vos exemplaria Graeca
nocturna versate manu, versate diurna
HORACE *A. P.* 268-269

ALTHOUGH *satura* in the Roman sense of the medley did not exist in Greece, yet there can be no difficulty in discovering what we should call satiric elements among Greek writers of all periods. Aristotle in the *Poetics* (iv. 7-8) points out how primitive a tendency it was among poets for some grave spirits to compose hymns to gods or eulogies on famous men and for other, less grave, spirits to compose invectives (ψόγους) against meaner persons. Such satirical attacks he sagely conjectures were probably plentiful even before Homer, but from Homer onward instances can be cited beginning with the *Margites*, which he names as a forerunner of comedy and which he wrongly accepts as Homeric. It was a later poem, partly in hexameters, partly in iambics, relating in coarse and laughable detail the adventures of a simpleton.[1] Aristotle could have gone back to genuine Homeric poetry for a sketch of character in which the ridiculous was stressed; for an excellent example in the *Iliad* is Thersites, the hunchback grumbler in the assembly of the Greek army before Troy, described as the most ill-favored man in the host; and in the *Odyssey* satiric color is exemplified in the incident of the windbags which Odysseus' companions unwisely opened and in his discomfiture when, after the resultant storm, he reappeared at the court of Aeolus, King of the Winds, vainly to ask for more, like an epic Oliver Twist![2] The epic hero tells the story against himself, a common artifice of satire.

Parody and burlesque are more developed forms of satire and presuppose a measure of literary criticism. We meet an early specimen in *The Battle of the Frogs and the Mice* (*Ba-*

[23]

trachomyomachia) which, assigned to Homer by uncritical ages, is, as we have it now in more than three hundred hexameters, perhaps an Attic reworking of a poem belonging to the Hesiodic period. It is an amusing travesty of the Homeric manner, peculiarly effective in the deliberations of Zeus and Athene about the divine part to be played in the coming war between frogs and mice, and entertaining in its details of the mock-epic struggle. The idea of a Council in heaven had a long history in satire: notable reappearances of this motif are found in Lucilius and in the *Pumpkinification of Claudius* by Seneca. The subject of dramatic burlesque of gods and heroes cannot here be followed up beyond drawing attention to the frequency of highly irreverent Sicilian comedies on mythological stories by Phormus or Phormis, Deinolochus, and Epicharmus. The last-named especially exercised influence on the satyr-drama of Athens, of which the sole surviving specimen is the *Cyclops* of Euripides. Another contribution from Sicily which may be mentioned in passing was that made by the mimes or mimic dialogues of Sophron. They were studied by Plato as models of vivacity to be imitated in his own dialogues, and thus through Plato influenced the mass of *Socraticae chartae* down to Hellenistic times, and in the last resort both Lucilius and Horace.

Satirizing in a personal manner was in Greek termed ἰαμβίζειν from the use of the iambus (ἴαμβος) in the meter of such attacks. On this side of satire three names stand out, Archilochus, Simonides, and Hipponax. By Archilochus iambic measures were directed virulently against Neobule, who had declined to marry him, and against her father. Like Juvenal, Archilochus found that rage begot verse: as Horace says, *Archilochum proprio rabies armavit iambo*.[3] These iambic Archilochian measures Horace declares with pride that he was the first to introduce into Latium,[4] that is to say, in his *Epodes*, several of which are in the broad sense satires, though not *saturae*. Besides invective force, Archilochus ex-

hibits another trait characteristic of satire, that of self-revelation: he recounts his quarrels, his recriminations against
friend and foe, his loose life, his throwing away of his shield
(*relicta non bene parmula*, as Horace says of himself in the
Odes).[5] From Simonides (or Semonides) of Amorgos we have
an iambic satire comparing women to sundry animals whose
natures they are unkindly alleged to share. He differs, however, from Juvenal in that he knew a good woman when he
saw her; for he includes a well-drawn picture of the blameless housewife who resembles the bee in industry and is a
gracious gift from Zeus to a husband.[6] Simonides borders on
the frontiers of the beast fable in his character sketches, as
Archilochus had done in stories about the fox. The prose beast
story, mainly imported from the East and in Greece traditionally ascribed to the Syrian or Phrygian "Aesop" as a re-
puted father of fable, always offered to the satirist useful
analogies for didactic purposes, and was freely employed in
the Cynic preaching, which we have yet to survey. It is a recurrent feature in Latin satire from Ennius onward, through
Horace's *Town Mouse and Country Mouse*, to the fables of
Phaedrus, some of whose bad beasts were recognized as too
slanderously similar to human beings. A third iambic poet,
Hipponax, retaliated in scurrilous verses on sculptors who
had exaggerated his deformity. This resembles the story illustrated in *Punch* by one of Phil May's drawings. An angry
woman entered a photographic studio and complained about
her husband's photographs. Asked what was wrong, she in-
dignantly declared, "My husband is exactly like an ape,"
and got the photographer's answer, "Well, Madam, you
ought to have thought of that before you had him 'taken.'"
So Hipponax perhaps ought to have thought twice before
he sanctioned any commissions for his bust or statue. Another point about him has importance. Besides using the ordinary iambic trimeter and tetrameter, he was especially
celebrated for his choliambic or "limping iambic" line end-

ing in a spondee, and employed by him for coarse abuse. It descends to Catullus and to Martial in Latin.

It was the comic dramatist Crates at Athens, Aristotle tells us,[7] who first dropped the mere satiric form (τῆς ἰαμβικῆς ἰδέας) and began to compose plots with a general application. This brings us to the dramatic trio Cratinus, Eupolis, and Aristophanes named by Horace as Lucilius' models.[8] With the amusement, or, as the Greeks called it, the "laughter" (γέλως) provoked by comedy they combined their object of reviling and chastising those whom they considered evildoers. Yet to sum up Aristophanes' plays as satires would obviously be to overlook his wealth of imaginative invention, his dramatic power, his gift of lyric sweetness. Satire in a comedy is a factor: it does not make the whole play.

Elsewhere too in Greek literature and Greek thought we find the satiric vein variously developed, thereby creating a tradition inherited in part by the satirists of Rome. This is especially noticeable in what was once a mass of ethical treatises drawing for their didactic aims from a wide stock of satirical devices in the presentment of their views, and often gilding the philosophical pill by humor in character drawing, in anecdote, or in fancy. This teaching of morality by satiric aids finds its way into poems of the *Greek Anthology*. It is a Hellenistic movement which creates a portion of the literary atmosphere breathed by the cultured members of the Scipionic Circle to which Lucilius belonged. This aspect of Hellenism is, therefore, apposite to our subject and must be appreciated in order rightly to estimate Lucilius as well as Horace, who borrowed freely from him. We owe to Geffcken valuable studies of this satiric element in Hellenic thought in his *Kynika und Verwandtes* and two contributions to *Neue Jahrbücher für das klassische Altertum* which he entitled *Studien zur griechischen Satire*. This second title uses the word "Satire" in a sense different from its Latin sense, and makes it do the work of some such phrase as "the satiric element" or "factor" or "principle" in Greece. It is thus a reminder that there is in Greek no word to express "satire" in the Roman specialized sense, while to express "satire" in the broader sense one would have to use γέλως or the late descriptive term for the blend of grave and gay, τὸ σπουδαιογέλοιον, and for the verb "satirize" one would have to use either ἰαμβίζειν or κωμῳδεῖν. Verbally, as well as materially, Quintilian was justified in his claim, *satura quidem tota nostra est.*

The once very extensive body of Hellenistic literature and thought which provided some of the roots for the growth of Roman satire has suffered much from the ravages of time. There have been within the last two generations valuable recoveries such as *Mimes* by Herondas and large portions of Menander's comedies; but a great part of the late Greek literature containing elements which influenced Roman satire is known to us mainly by quotations in still later writers with occasional reënforcement through modern finds. A pertinent example is that of Phoenix of Colophon, whose choliambics were known previously through five quotations in Athenaeus,[9] but about whose satiric outlook on life increased knowledge has been gained through the recovery in recent times of verses of his, preserved, though in a mutilated condition, on papyrus.[10]

Into this varied, though partly elusive literature, we cannot enter in full detail lest we should be tempted to dwell too long by the sources, actual or possible, of Roman satire, and neglect the great river which flowed therefrom.[11] But before noting some of its prevailing characteristics and ideas and some of its leading names, we may find an apposite introduction in two passages from Horace. The first occurs in the longest and best constructed of Horace's *Satires*, the third of the second book, published in 30 B.C. In two lines there (11-12), Horace gives a brief list of holiday reading for a

Roman satirist, namely, the books taken away in reality or in imagination—it hardly matters which—for his own winter vacation in the country at his recently acquired Sabine farm, where he hopes to escape the rowdy festivities of the Saturnalian season. He makes his friend Damasippus twit him with sloth in writing, and ask, supposing he were to produce no more satires, "What was the point of packing Plato with Menander, and bringing from town those weighty companions, Eupolis and Archilochus?" This is an instructive selection of Greek authors from whom material for a *satura* could be drawn. Here Plato, if Orelli is correct in taking him for the philosopher, would represent ethical thought; or, if he is Plato the playwright of the Middle Attic Comedy, then he would be a link between the Old Comedy of Eupolis and the New Comedy of Menander, who is mentioned next to him. To the fourth name, Archilochus, the iambic satirist, allusion has already been made.

The other passage, in the second book of the *Epistles*,[12] remarks on the different tastes of readers in poetry, one pleased with lyric (*carmine*), his neighbor with epodes or *iambi*, a third with satire, which is characterized as "Bionean causeries and their caustic wit" (*Bioneis sermonibus et sale nigro*). This significantly regards Bion as a representative of satire, and, though Horace did not copy the mordancy of Bion's wit, his debt to the diatribes was considerable and must be mentioned in connection with the Cynic teaching of Hellenistic times.

The preoccupation with philosophy was more marked and more widely spread in Greece than in Rome. The philosophy of conduct, however, seemed practical enough to interest many Romans; and Roman satire, as a social organ, was intimately concerned therewith. *Socraticae chartae* (Socratic writings or papers), a general term for Greek ethical treatises or discourses, was a significant phrase used by Horace, and, in a masculine form, by Lucilius before him. From the Socratico-Platonic stock sprang Cynicism or Cynism, which, though aiming like Stoicism at achieving the ideal of self-sufficiency (αὐτάρκεια), was a more absolute negation of the appeal of society. The Cynic, in large measure a law unto himself, defied convention with a rude arrogance and sometimes with the snarls which earned him the nickname of "dog" (κύων). Cynism was in effect a self-centered, nonsocial mode of thought. Unlike Stoicism, which was a creed for the cultured, Cynicism appealed to the malcontent and the poor: it was the Stoicism of the unfortunate. The Cynic missioner, affecting a Diogenes-like contempt for outward appearance, conveyed his propaganda not in formal lectures but in talks, διατριβαί, *sermones*, *causeries*.[13] Much of his oratory was never written down. He was essentially a street preacher, for whom abstruse problems and paradoxes had to give place to practical counsels in life. His basis was reality: vice and wrong had to be fought in the breach. The evils of society offered just such a popular theme, bound up with the inordinate pursuit of riches; and the transition from the subject of riches to that of vice is illustrated in the fragments of Bion[14] and particularly in his influence upon the first satire of Horace's first book.[15]

But there was a lighter side to the didactic methods of Cynic moralists. Mere violence of denunciation did not achieve the results sought after. A Diogenes found that the people at large did not so much listen to his doctrine as laugh at his jests. The more the Cynic preacher tempered his oratory, the more did the jocular win a place alongside of earnestness. Here the mythic element was of service in providing something light, and fable had the merit of uniting the simple and the conversational with the didactic. The Bionean diatribe, attractive in its variety and freedom, is accordingly classed as an outstanding example of τὸ σπουδαιο-γέλοιον, the "jocular-earnest," where it was not so much a case of the importance of being earnest as of the importance

of being entertaining in one's earnest. Among attractions in
this sort of exhortation an important part was played by
the poetic rhythm which held a hearer and impressed itself
on his memory. Crates, the Cynic, not the comic dramatist,
emphasized the value of poetic form in philosophical discourses: and Stoics as well as Cynics cultivated the practice
of quoting from well-known poets, or adapting or even parodying a poet's words, or inserting verses of their own (as we
find is done by Seneca in his *Apocolocyntosis*, and later by
Martianus Capella and Boethius).

A glance at some prominent topics or commonplaces will
illustrate this philosophic preaching and at the same time a
good many pristine elements of Roman satire. Attacks upon
riches and covetousness are found, as indicated, in surviving
pieces by Phoenix of Colophon. Social customs, as a whole,
fell under a Cynic's scrutiny, especially those fostering vice.
True to the Stoic affinity of the school, a Cynic denounced
drunkenness as being in conflict with nature, while water
drinking could claim the sanction of living according to nature. The proper attitude toward the caprices of fortune is a
favorite theme: wise adaptation to circumstances is coun-
seled in Teles, and complaints about one's lot (μεμψιμοιρία),
one of the subjects of the first satire in Horace, is exposed as
folly. Life is a theatrical stage and men merely players: they
should ungrudgingly take the part assigned to them in the
drama of life, as an actor takes it in a play. It is best to meet
evils with complete indifference(ἀπάθεια); and, after all, evils
might be proved by philosophy to be no evils. The nothingness of life is stressed by Menippus as he is represented in
Lucian: his Cynic demand to know where are all the famed
beauties of the past in the world of the dead anticipates by
many centuries Villon's *Ballade des dames du temps jadis:*

> Dictes-moy où, n'en quel pays,
> Est Flora, la belle Romaine? ...
> Mais où sont les neiges d'antan?

Yes, "where are the snows of yesteryear?" Such themes are endless; for the outlook is on the greatest comedy of all, human life, its eternal masquerade of all sorts and conditions of men. Fair game for a mocker can always be found in dinner parties, table luxuries, legacy hunting, quarrels, and philosophies. We have them in Greek as afterward in Latin.

It is impossible here to discuss the long series of Greeks who exhibited in different ways the satiric spirit.[16] Followers of Diogenes like Philiskos, Kerkidas, and Monimos (the author of "sportive trifles blended with a latent seriousness"),[17] followers of Zeno like Poseidippos of Alexandria and Dionysios from the Pontic Heracleia, as well as the Skeptic Timon of Phlius, may be mentioned in passing, and others must be omitted. The variety of Crates' use of different meters deserves attention; and the scazons or choliambics of Phoenix have been indicated as typically moralizing in tone. Herondas in the middle of the third century made the mimiambos his speciality for dialogues of realistic power, as we can see since the recovery of mimes of his from a mutilated papyrus in Egypt in 1891. The choliambic had its own separate history in Latin not only in Catullus and Martial and in Varro's Menippean Satires, but also in Petronius (ch. 5), in Persius' prologue, and later in Boethius.[18] In the iambics of Crantor we meet one of the recurrent complaints against poverty, which I may render:

> No lot in life can be more miserable
> Than poverty. Noble your soul may be,
> Yet, if you're poor, you will be laughed to scorn.

> (οὐκ ἔστι πενίας οὐδὲν ἀθλιώτερον
> ἐν τῷ βίῳ σύμπτωμα· καὶ γὰρ ἂν φύσει
> σπουδαῖος ᾖς, πένης δέ, καταγέλως ἔσει.)

It is like Juvenal's lines in *Satires* III 152-153:

> nil habet infelix paupertas durius in se
> quam quod ridiculos homines facit:

for which Johnson, in his adaptation "London," gave the well-known version:

> Of all the griefs that harass the distress'd
> Sure the most bitter is a scornful jest.

The employment of so many verse-forms—hexameter, elegiac, iambic, choliambic, trochaic tetrameter, and sotadean measure—to carry satiric ideas is worth noting as a partial explanation of Lucilius' experiments in various meters before he finally concentrated on the hexameter.

Leonidas of Tarentum may be cited[19] to illustrate the influence of the diatribe on the thought of poems contained in the *Anthology*: he comments satirically on the folly of the high hopes of man for whom the worm waits. One of the predominantly Cynic τόποι, the pessimistic note on the vanity and transience of human life, is expressed in a fragment ascribed to Menander which may be thus translated:

> Wouldst know thyself for what thou truly art?
> Glance at the tombstones as thou farest forth.
> There lie but bones and trivial dust of kings
> That were, and princes and philosophers,
> And those who plumed themselves on rank and wealth,
> Upon their fame, or on their handsome looks.
> But nought thereof saved them from cruel Time.
> The world beyond is shared by every man:
> Let this glance teach thee how thyself to scan.

> (ὅταν εἰδέναι θέλῃς σεαυτὸν ὅστις εἶ,
> ἐμβλεψον εἰς τὰ μνήμαθ', ὡς ὁδοιπορεῖς.
> ἐνταῦθ' ἔνεστ' ὀστᾶ τε καὶ κούφη κόνις
> ἀνδρῶν βασιλέων καὶ τυράννων καὶ σοφῶν
> καὶ μέγα φρονούντων ἐπὶ γένει καὶ χρήμασιν
> αὐτῶν τε δόξῃ κἀπὶ κάλλει σωμάτων.
> ἀλλ' οὐδὲν αὐτοῖς τῶνδ' ἐπήρκεσεν χρόνον.[20]
> κοινὸν τὸν ἄδην ἔσχον οἱ πάντες βροτοί.
> πρὸς ταῦθ' ὁρῶν γίνωσκε σαυτὸν ὅστις εἶ.)

It should be noted that the maxim γνῶθι σεαυτὸν ("Know thyself") is the title of one of Varro's Satires.

Bion's relation to Horace has been mentioned, and a few additional remarks may be made on the man and his works. Bion of Borysthenes, once a slave, occupied himself with the study of different systems of philosophy at Athens. If in the main Cynic, his own creed was relatively independent. Scraps of his wit and wisdom are recorded by Teles; but it may be assumed that Teles, after the ancient fashion, has far oftener incorporated the sayings of Bion than he acknowledges by mentioning his original.[21] We find traces of his interest in his own personality—touches of autobiography which anticipate the frank avowal *libertino patre natum* of Horace. He treats with indifference snobbish prejudices directed against himself or his forebears, or can answer them with the wit which made his fame. Even against man's last enemy he has his jest: "The way to death is easy and smooth: one can go with eyes shut!"[22] This grim humor is true to the conception of the σπουδαιογέλοιον.

There remains one name of signal importance in connection with the satires of Varro—that of Menippus, the Cynic from Gadara in the first half of the third century B.C. Originally from a Semitic town, Menippus was yet typically Greek. We can discern much of his attitude to life indirectly through the Syrian satirist Lucian, who imitated him and introduced him as a figure in several of his books in the second century A.D. As Helm[23] has shown, a fair conception of at least part of the Menippean attitude can be gained by grouping together the Hades scenes from the *Necyomanteia, Cataplous,* and *The Dialogues of the Dead* of Lucian.

Born in slavery, Menippus bought his freedom and became a pupil of the Cynic Metrocles. The satires called after his name were philosophic *feuilletons* of a Cynic strain with interspersed verses. This blend of verse and prose was also a blend of the grave and gay, the caustic humor making

Menippus'work an excellent representative of the σπουδαιογέλοιον. In his celebrated piece, the Νέκυια, he imitated
Crates; and was in his particular genre imitated in turn by
Meleagros of Gadara in the first century B.C. and by Lucian
in the second century A.D.

It is useless to expect to get a detailed conception of the
art of the Gadarene satirist from the adaptations by a writer
of such independent originality as Lucian. But if we cannot
recover his style, we have definitely Lucian's picture of
Menippus and in it we can recognize much of what Menippus meant and thought, and how existence was conceived of
by a genius that was earnest even though it laughed at the
folly of men. Lucian was "dramatist" enough, sufficiently
master of realistic dialogue, to make Menippus speak true
to character when he introduces him. Hence it is highly significant to note the utterances which Lucian puts into Menippus' mouth in his writings, and particular value attaches
to the sketch entitled *Menippus* or *Necyomanteia* (The Oracle
of the Dead). Menippus there is imagined to relate the story
of his descent into Hades. Starting with quotations from
Homer and Euripides, he explains that he has been impelled
to undertake his journey because of his dissatisfaction with
the different philosophies of the world and their contradictory futilities. A Babylonian wizard—and here we get a touch
of Eastern mysticism added to Hellenic mythology—has
guided him into the land of shades. What follows is a parody of Greek lore concerning the Stygian lake. While the
souls of the dead make lamentation, Menippus characteris-
tically is amused and laughs. He sees judgments being passed
upon the ghosts of human offenders brought before the tribunal of Minos. The note of social satire appears in the very
list of the prisoners bound with a long chain and still more
in the brief comments made upon them—"adulterers and
procurers, farmers of the revenues, and flatterers and informers, and a similar company of such as disturb everything

in men's existence (τοιοῦτος ὅμιλος τῶν πάντα κυκώντων ἐν
τῷ βίῳ): and apart there came forward the rich and exactors
of usury, pale, fat-paunched and gouty."

Especial severity, he notes, is shown in punishing pride of
wealth and power. This condemnation of the rich is comparable with the Teles-Bion criticism of excessive wealth which
influenced Horace. On the one hand, Menippus takes a cynical delight in beholding arrogance humiliated, and a mischievous joy in reminding the ghosts of their vanished earthly
glories. On the other hand, his social sympathies are evident
in his record of the leniency shown to the poor. The typical
humor of Cynicism appears in the insistence upon the like-
ness of all ghosts and the difficulty of distinguishing former
beauties from ugly folk, a beggar from a king, a cook from
Agamemnon. In passing, one ought to observe the obvious
inconsistencies inherent in all descriptions of the Underworld. If at times the dead are said to be indistinguishable,
at other times Menippus is fancied to find no difficulty in
recognizing personages and different classes of people.

It is well worth while to illustrate Lucian's account of
Menippus' reflections upon human existence as resembling
a processional pageant, because it conveys a good deal of his
Cynic attitude and of ideas familiar in Roman satire. From
the extract[24] which I translate we may derive a notion of
what some of the lost satires of Varro were like:

So, in good truth, as I looked thereupon, the life of mankind
appeared to me to resemble some long procession.[25] And Fortune
(ἡ τύχη), methought, had to equip and arrange every particular,
apportioning to those in the procession costumes different and
variegated. One she would take and furnish in regal style, setting on him a tiara, assigning him bodyguards, and crowning
his head with the diadem. Another she would clothe in the dress
of a menial. A third she would decorate in beauty; and a fourth
she would turn out deformed, a figure of fun; for the show, I imagine, must needs be of all sorts and conditions.

And often, in the midst of the procession, she would alter the raiment of some, and not permit them to go through it to the end, as they had been arranged, but exchanging the garb of a Croesus she forced him to assume the dress of a servant and a captive; while a Maeandrius, hitherto marching among slaves, she invested with the despotic power of a Polycrates, and up to a certain point permitted him to wear the royal garb. But when the time of the procession had passed, at that moment each one abandoned his equipment and, putting off his costume with his body, became just as he was before, no whit different from his neighbor.

Now some, from folly ($\upsilon\pi'$ $\dot{\alpha}\gamma\nu\omega\mu\sigma\sigma\dot{\nu}\nu\eta\varsigma$), as soon as Fortune stands over them and demands back her decorations, are vexed and indignant, as though they were being deprived of property of their own, and as if they were not restoring what they had the use of for a brief space.

Among players on the stage I imagine you have often seen these tragic actors who, to meet the requirements of the dramas, become now Creons, now Priams or Agamemnons; and the same man, if so it chance, who a little before represented very impressively ($\sigma\epsilon\mu\nu\tilde{\omega}\varsigma$) the bearing of a Cecrops or an Erechtheus, soon afterward comes forward as a servant on the summons of the poet. And when the play is over, each of them divests himself of that gold-embroidered raiment, puts aside his mask, descends from the tragic buskins, and walks about as a poor and humble person, no longer Agamemnon, son of Atreus, nor yet Creon, son of Menoeceus, but called Polus, son of Charicles from Sunium, or Satyrus, son of Theogiton, from Marathon.

After this fashion, truly, go the affairs of men, as they then appeared to my eyes.

When the passage is examined, it is clear that many commonplaces of Cynic preaching are suggested—the caprice of fortune; ups and downs in life; the folly of grumbling over hardships; possessions as temporary, not permanent; all the world as a stage and men and women merely players; death as a leveler at the close.

In Lucian's *Icaromenippus* ("Menippus the Flier") the wings of comedy, as in the *Birds* of Aristophanes, have carried us through the air from the underworld of the *Necyomanteia* to the gods above. This sketch is thoroughly Menippean in spirit, though Lucian has combined, in the true satiric tradition, elements of fun from the Old Comedy. The humor is soon felt by a reader: we have laughable prayer tubes on the one hand, and on the other the impious wishes of men against the life of a neighbor, as in Horace (*Epist*. I. xvi. 57 sqq.) and in the tenth satire of Juvenal. Much in Lucian's *Council of the Gods* and *Zeus as Tragedian* must, like the idea of the *Deorum Concilium* in the first book of Lucilius and of Seneca's *Apocolocyntosis*, go back to Menippus.

What general picture can we draw of this clever critic of life? Pugnacious, and by his pugnacity arousing aversion, Menippus yet viewed with complacency the hostility which his outspokenness called forth. Indeed, he conformed to a persistent trait of a satirist in feeling his own personality to be important and therefore making a frank revelation of it. He is interested in recording his own combative experiences, much as Varro in his *Eumenides* tells of a prosecution out of which he had triumphantly emerged. Still, though he started from Cynicism as a base, he is not an absolute philosophic partisan: in fact, it is clear that, like his contemporary, Leonidas of Tarentum,[26] he could make fun of certain Cynics. Not wholly intolerant, he mocked at specious sectaries and held dogmatic philosophers up to ridicule. But, as Geffcken points out, he is no Timon: he has a well-developed satiric interest in the whole of human life, and his laughter is tempered with melancholy. His theme is the wide one of Juvenal's *quicquid agunt homines*. But the whole swarm of mankind—kings, soldiers, teachers, athletes, rich and poor, and pests of society like usurers, procurers, legacy hunters—alike in his eyes needed guidance. What, therefore, Epicureanism attempted through gentle teaching, Menippus attempted through jests and gibes, behind which lurked earnest. It is to show how foolish is the dread of death and how empty

the passion for earthly fame that he embarks in the skiff of
Charon and laughs unrestrainedly in the lower world. His
method of dealing with popular belief or superstition is not
to argue, as Lucretius did, seriously and systematically, but
to confront the mythological figures, to scoff at them, to dispel
the whole illusion. They are, Charon included, made absurd,
and the mythological dream is broken. In Lucian's *Dialogues
of the Dead*, when Menippus flippantly makes the unheard-
of refusal to pay his fare for his passage across the Styx,
Charon gets the worse of the altercation. He exclaims in-
dignantly to Hermes, the conductor of the dead, "Where
did you bring this dog from?" and is astounded at "the sort
of things he babbled on the passage, laughing and jeering at
all the passengers: he was the only one singing while they
were making lament" (οἷα δὲ καὶ ἐλάλει παρὰ τὸν πλοῦν
τῶν ἐπιβατῶν ἁπάντων καταγελῶν καὶ ἐπισκώπτων καὶ μόνος
ᾄδων οἰμωζώντων ἐκείνων). But the jesting singer aimed at
conveying the serious admonition that mankind must not
tremble before meaningless shadows or be hoodwinked by
idle shows. Man must stand firm upon reality. Such was one
of the lessons taught by Menippean satire: while it could
amuse, it could also instruct.

The literary history of satire in Latin begins for us with
Ennius; for, though Naevius showed a satiric bent in comedy, there is no proof that he wrote independent satires. The
grammarian Diomedes[27] in the fourth century A.D., after declaring that in his day *satira* meant a *carmen* which attacked
vice after the way of the Old Comedy and was represented
by Lucilius, Horace, and Persius, proceeds to illustrate the
old *satira* consisting of different poems (*quod ex variis poematibus constabat*) by stating that this was the sort written
by Pacuvius and Ennius (*quale scripserunt Pacuvius et Ennius*). The order of the two names is not chronological; for
Pacuvius was Ennius' nephew. Indeed an epigram[28] professedly by Pompilius calls Pacuvius a pupil (*discipulus*) of

Ennius, which may mean he was inspired to emulate Ennius in tragedy, and possibly in satire, too, though nothing remains of his satires. But to Ennius' satires, reduced to scraps as they now are,[29] many allusions are made. Quintilian[30] mentions his introducing a wrangle between the personified figures of Life and Death in one of his satires (*Mortem et Vitam quas contendentes in satura tradit Ennius*). Gellius[31] quotes four lines with a curious word-play on *frustrari* and *frustra* which he says occur in Ennius' satires (*qui sunt in Saturis Q. Enni*); and in another passage[32] he records the Ennian spelling *memorderit*, not *momorderit* (*Q. Ennius in Saturis "memorderit" dixit per "e" literam, non "momorderit"*). Donatus and Servius, Nonius and Macrobius are more explicit; for they make quotations from specified books —I, II, III, or IV, as the case may be—of what they each call the *Saturae* of Ennius. In spite of this considerable body of evidence, Marx is skeptical about the title, and suggests that Ennius styled this part of his writings *poemata per saturam*.[33] Donatus in a comment upon a passage in Terence[34] seems to cite a sixth book, but the reading may be in error; for Porphyrio on Horace *Satires* I. x. 46 declares that Ennius left four books of satires. The surviving fragments conform to the meaning of the title as a medley; for they are in a variety of meters—iambic, trochaic, and hexameter—and include fables, dialogues, and comments on life in a light manner which contrasts with the elevation of the author's tragic and epic style.

Ennius, who was born at Rudiae in Calabria in 239 B.C., died in 169 B.C. at the age of seventy years. It is likely that his satires, of which the third book contains an allusion to Scipio's services,[35] were written after the triumph celebrated by Scipio in 201 B.C. in honor of the final contests of the second Punic War. The suggestion, however, that the poem entitled *Scipio* in the list of his works should be reckoned among the satires, has not won general support; nor is Lucian Müller's view[36] generally accepted that they included his didactic *Epicharmus*, the gastronomic *Hedyphagetica* (a sort of handbook to "Delicatessen"), the *Ambracia*, *Euhemerus*, *Protreptica*, *Sota*, and his Epigrams. But certainly among his trochaic *Saturae* was the delightful fable of the crested lark (*de avicula cassita*) and her young, retold in prose by Gellius[37] to illustrate the unwisdom of trusting to others for work which you can better do for yourself. The fable is in the Aesopian manner, which the diatribe had found useful to convey a lesson. A lark had its nest in a cornfield and toward harvest time her young were scarcely able to fly. One day, when the mother bird had flown away in search of food, the nestlings overheard the farmer telling his son, as the corn was ripe, to go and summon a few friends to help in cutting next day. The young birds in great alarm entreated their mother on her return to remove them at once into a safe place. She, however, is undisturbed. "If the master," she remarks, "entrusts the reaping to friends, it will not be done tomorrow." Next day the mother flew away again for food. The sun was bright, but no "friends" came. So the master says to his son, "These friends are very slow: let us ask our relations to come early tomorrow." Overhearing this, the nestlings again suffer their panic and inform their mother on her arrival home. Her comment is, "No relations are so obliging as to comply at once with such a request." But on the third day the farmer is overheard saying to his son, "Goodbye to friends and relations: bring a pair of sickles at dawn: I'll take one; you'll take the other. We'll reap the corn with our own hands." The moment this was told to her, the mother bird decided, "The time has come for us to go."

Ennius, says Gellius, told this apologue from Aesop in his *saturae* with remarkable skill and beauty in tetrameters. The remark which Gellius adds may be translated thus: "The two concluding lines, I feel strongly, it is well worth while to keep in the heart and memory:

'This shall be your working maxim, and you'll always find it true:
Never look to friends for doing what yourself you well can do'."

> (*Hoc erit tibi argumentum semper in promptu situm:
> ne quid exspectes amicos quod tute agere possies.*)

Ennius, gravely dignified in tragedy and epic, did not possess the sparkling wit requisite to make him a master in comedy; but that he had a gift of quiet humor the preceding fable teaches. One of his humorous pictures, represented now by a single mock-heroic trochaic line, portrays a flute player who thought he could catch sea fish by piping to them:

> Once a piper took his station hard by Ocean's wide expanse.

> (*Subulo quondam marinas propter astabat plagas.*)

The notorious tmesis or splitting of the inseparable parts of the Latin word *cerebrum*, "brain," in *saxo cere comminuit brum* is ascribed to him by an old commentator on Donatus.[38] It is equivalent to saying in English "With a stone his *bra*-he smashed *-in*." This seems too much for some scholars to accept as by Ennius. Yet he might have been whimsical enough to introduce it into one of his *saturae*: he might indeed have been making fun of tmesis by reducing it *ad absurdum*. Even Ennius might unbend; and critics who were cynically described by a great British statesman as "men who have failed in literature and art" are not necessarily unerring judges of the way of a genius with a word.

The graver side of Ennius' nature must not blind us to his claim that he possessed three hearts (*tria corda*)—a Greek, an Oscan, and a Latin heart.[39] As a Southerner and by education he was especially subjected to Greek influences, and this fact lends color to the view that he was "grafting the Sicilian mime on the coarser but kindred stock of Roman *satura*."[40] His interest in Epicharmus is shown in his trochaic miscellany of the philosophic thought of the old Sicilian playwright, and hereby Ennius bequeathed to Roman

satire a tradition of the popular preaching of philosophy as
a way of life instead of abstract theorizing, while his *Euhemerus*, apparently in prose, showed his tendency to ration-
alize myths—afterward an element in the satires of Horace.
The *Hedyphagetica*, whether a *satura* or not, marks the first
appearance in Latin of a common topic in Roman satire, the
science and art of dietetics. It was based on a Sicilian poem
by Archestratus of Gela. This theme of right or wrong feeding descended from the Pythagoreans, who were notorious
champions of vegetarianism; and its literary treatment had
roots in the mime, where the learned doctor and professional
cook were sometimes half comically, but also most sensibly,
made identical. The influence of this topic on Horace is seen
in the second and the fourth satires of his second book. In
the former (II. ii), simple diet is seriously advocated:[41] in
the latter (II. iv), luxurious feeding is ironically described;
for the satirists of Rome enter *con amore* into a mock-heroic
portrayal of rich banquets to be regarded by the sapient as
awful examples and salutary warnings. "I remember," says
Catius to Horace,[42] "the very teaching which I am now to
recite" (*ipsa memor praecepta canam*): so by a pleasant fiction he pretends to convey professorial rules on the art of
dining well.

One other aspect of Ennius' influence merits notice. His
experiments with different meters, including the hexameter,
in his *Saturae*, were taken up by Lucilius, whose preference,
after trial duly made, for the hexameter[43] determined the
verse-form of normal Latin satire.

CHAPTER III

LUCILIUS, CREATOR OF THE ROMAN TYPE

Secuit Lucilius urbem
PERSIUS I. 114

THE NAME of Lucilius is a great one in the chronicle of Roman satire, for several reasons. He it was who, with his endowment of vigorous expression, imparted to the *satura* a spirit in great measure renounced by Horace but renewed by Juvenal; he reflected the Greek culture of the Scipionic Circle, but was earnestly, almost violently, interested in the Roman society and politics of his day; he combined erudition with everyday language and the plain style approved by Stoics and adaptable to his mordancy; he, by force of example, made the hexameter the standard meter for Latin satire; he influenced Horace deeply; and the range of theme and of expression within his compass, which can be deduced from his fragments, as well as his power of vivid portrayal and that open self-revelation to which Horace bears testimony,[1] make the loss of his works one of the grievous blanks in the literary history of Rome. We have now no passage of his longer than the thirteen rather dull lines on Virtue, and so many of his scraps are saved to us because they were cited by grammarians, especially Nonius Marcellus, merely for the sake of some strange word or usage, that it is difficult to estimate him fairly as a stylist. It is also hard to understand why, long after Horace's insistence upon his uncouth carelessness in composition,[2] there were Roman readers, Quintilian says,[3] who declared him to be their favorite among all poets, while others with an archaistic bias specified, according to Tacitus,[4] their preference for him over Horace as they did for Lucretius over Virgil.

Lucilius was born at Suessa Aurunca, on the Campanian border toward Latium. As he served at Numantia under Scipio in 134-133 B.C., it is usually agreed that the date 148

[43]

B.C. obtainable from Jerome for his birth year is much too late. The most satisfactory rectification is to suppose that Jerome confused the consuls of that year with the similarly named ones of 180.[5] Cichorius prefers 157 or 167. Lucilius' death is now usually referred to 102, and his literary activity to the thirty years preceding. A member of an Italian family of wealth and standing, at Rome he was made welcome in the Scipionic Circle, the group of Roman nobles and of literary men associated with the younger Scipio Africanus Aemilianus and Laelius surnamed "the Wise" (*Sapiens*). They formed a friendly coterie of moderately progressive politicians and lovers of Greek culture. It is recorded that Lucilius settled in the house that had been built at Rome for the hostage son of Antiochus the Great.[6] The atmosphere in which he moved was one of the best Hellenic erudition; for Cicero says of P. Africanus, C. Laelius, and L. Furius that they "constantly and publicly kept in their company the most learned men from Greece" (*secum eruditissimos homines ex Graecia palam semper habuerunt*),[7] and elsewhere he makes Laelius remark on Scipio's preëminence "in what I might call our set" (*in nostro, ut ita dicam, grege*).[8]

Roman history provides the notorious spectacle of a Hellenism now frowned on by opponents like Cato as a pernicious element of effeminacy and corruption, and now welcomed by others like Scipio as a broadening system of cosmopolitan culture. It had already found encouragement in the generation of the elder Africanus and of L. Aemilius Paullus, though this does not imply that we should extend the phrase "Scipionic Circle" to include the forerunners of the younger Scipio.[9] These earlier days were those of Ennius, who in his epic, the *Annales*, had given utterance to the spirit of the nation which defeated Carthage. If time had spared Ennius' satires, we should have expected from them more light upon the social conditions of his age. In the days of the younger Scipio we reach a fresh period which seemed to invite a satirist. It was permeated with a ferment of new ideas, and impelled toward criticism of private and public life by the growth of social and political discontent. Greek philosophy too made its contribution toward an analysis of existing conditions in the state; for the Stoic theories of Blossius of Cumae had an influence on the Gracchan agitation which is not to be overlooked. The second half of the second century B.C. was one of the most troubled in Roman history. The period saw the opening of Rome's imperial dominion and of difficulties the solution of which did not come till the settlement under Augustus. A victorious control of the Western Mediterranean by Rome meant the demoralizing enrichment of a favored few but widespread misery and economic distress for many. Attempts to restore equilibrium tended in large part to accentuate the contrast between rich and poor. Neither Gracchan legislative measures nor sumptuary laws succeeded in meeting social evils; and the political struggles of the time were at root economic. When Lucilius, then, derides the multiplication of luxuries he is not merely repeating Stoic attacks upon wealth and serving up Greek platitudes. Since he realized that the indecent display of riches is an insult to poverty, his satire was calculated to claim better conditions of life for the majority.

Another historical fact pregnant with permanent results was the closer contact with the Orient and particularly with Greek culture. This inevitably involved alterations in time-honored Roman customs, beliefs, and education. Ways of thinking and modes of expression could for those once under the influence of Hellenism never quite move again in the same groove. This cultural influence is best exemplified in the entourage of Scipio. The Scipionic Circle included men of a practical outlook on affairs—orators, lawyers, and soldiers —so that intercourse within it meant no mere bookish pedantry, but a training in the problems of actual life. Conversation, an art fostered by its members, turned at least as much on moral and political as on literary and linguistic subjects; and here we see the source of much in Lucilius. On the literary side the Circle had notable figures in him and Terence; and among Greek adherents were Panaetius, the philosopher from Rhodes, and Polybius, the Achaean states-man whose devotion to Roman history bore fruit in a de-servedly famous work. In befriending Terence the Circle hon-ored itself. His African origin possibly was an initial and appropriate recommendation in the eyes of the younger Afri-canus; but his own literary gift of refinement in drama, from the appearance of his first play in 166 onward, manifestly captured the taste of the cultured set, although it failed to hold the generality of people in the face of rival attractions. Here, then, was an opening for Lucilius, who could best at-tract readers by showering a rain of satiric comment upon contemporary life in language which was direct and Roman in its ring. To an appreciable degree he was the mouthpiece of the Circle. Entering it, he took over its culture, its social views, even its stock of political animus to furnish forth his writing. Scipio's enemies were his enemies and his butts; so he dislikes the marriage laws of Scipio's opponent Q. Cae-cilius Metellus Numidicus, censor in 131 B.C.; and, what sounds a finer testimony from Horace, Lucilius was kindly only to Virtue and to Virtue's friends.[10]

Panaetius, the great philosopher of the group, exerted a potent influence not only within the Scipionic Circle, but also posthumously upon Cicero and upon Horace. By his sensible modification of the more extravagant doctrines of Stoicism he won the adherence of Romans who were able to unite the best traditions of Rome and Greece. The idea of *humanitas*,[11] colored with Hellenic feeling, reached an acme of significance in the systems of Panaetius and his followers Antiochus and Posidonius. For them and for the Scipionic Circle it em-braced more than a theoretical φιλανθρωπία: it involved a recognition of all men as parts of one great organism, and with the sense of common membership in a world-state it aimed at combining a high degree of individual culture. Terence's line, put in the mouth of Chremes, "I'm human: what's a man's affair is mine" (*homo sum: humani nil a me alienum puto*) is typical of a genuine breadth of outlook, and would also serve as a fit motto for the wide range of Lucilian satire. Yet there is a measure of ferocity in many of Lucilius' strictures which seems so incompatible with the amiable courtesy of Panaetius' ideal that one wonders what his satire might have become without the tempering influence of the Greek thinker. To Cicero *humanitas* on its kindlier side made a stronger appeal. He could accept for his treatise *On Duties* (*De Officiis*) the major portion of Panaetius' modified Stoicism. Cicero was keenly alive to the bonds uniting human society[12] and to the *benevolentia* and *mansuetudo* implied in a true *humanitas*. Not everything in satire would have met with his approbation; for just as he liked the "liberal jest," that is, the fun which a gentleman would sanction, and, just as he enjoyed polite conversation, so he revolted against the Cynics' boorish defiance of use and custom as an offense against that modesty and reverence, that *verecundia*, which is a presupposition in morality. For Cicero, as for Horace, the *decorum* which Panaetius inculcated as τὸ πρέπον weighed heavily both in literature and in conduct.[13] Horace is nearer to the Ciceronian conception of jest than to the Lucilian. The elegant jest in Cicero's view is becoming to a dignified person, the other sort, being vulgar, is "illiberal" —unworthy of a freeborn man (*ingenuus*). This sort of humor Cicero finds in comedy and in books of Socratic philosophy, which to him illustrate wit and irony at their best. The Ciceronian theory, based on the Panaetian and so an inheritance from the Scipionic Circle, is expounded by him in connection with self-control in such passions as rage, and in connection with amusement or relaxation.[14] Jest is conceded its rightful place in life. A very proper change from serious pursuits, it must not be immoderate, but refined and witty (*ingenuum et facetum*). So for conversation as an art, that is to say *sermo*, the famous word in both Lucilius and Horace, Cicero would refer to the Socratics as the most excellent patterns.[15] *Sermo*, he urges, should be easy and not at all dogmatic (*pertinax*): it should be grave or gay according to the subject. Care should be taken not to risk betraying faults in one's own character by the manner of one's conversation, and (a point insisted on by Horace) ill-natured and slanderous statements about the absent should be avoided. Extreme censoriousness would not therefore be approved either in conversation or in satire, and we know how Horace rejects it as unlikely to be reformative in effect. Lucilius, however, being more akin to the Cynics, indulged more freely in invective than would be permitted by Panaetius to the liberal jest. But he regarded his works as "talks," *sermones*, with his mind partly on the Cynic διατριβή, but perhaps also partly on actual discussions with intimates which gave him rough material for his writing. Possibly, too, if he read these *causeries* within his literary circle, the pretension to no more formal a description than *sermones* might seem to mitigate the intensity of his satire. Yet by preference his tendencies took him back through the popular teachers of Cynicism to the outspoken Old Comedy, in the spirit of which he delivered his uncompromising attacks upon the entire city (*primores populi arripuit populumque tributim.*)[16] He showed his real quality in vehemence rather than in that urbane restraint[17] which aided Horace's *curiosa felicitas* in language. The savant in him had equipment of salted words.

The surviving fragments of Lucilius number nearly fourteen hundred lines or scraps of lines—a very imperfect representation of his total work, which consisted of thirty books. On these extant passages and fragments, on their interpretation and possible context, on their connection, if any, with other fragments, an immense amount of scholarship has been bestowed from the time of the *editio princeps* issued in 1597 by Dousa—a remarkable performance for a young man of twenty. In the forties of last century some progress was made in Corpet's edition with French translation and notes (1845) and Gerlach's (1846). The seventies brought a little more light in Lucian Müller's edition (1872) and Lachmann's (1876). Baehrens included a text in his *Fragmenta Poetarum Romanorum* of 1886. But a great advance came in this twentieth century. Marx's Leipzig edition of the *Reliquiae* with his valuable *Prolegomena* and commentary in two volumes (1904-1905) was epoch-making. It was rich in parallel material, and suggestive, though overdaring, in its ingenious endeavor to connect hitherto isolated fragments. On Marx several scholars have since built.[18] Valuable contributions to knowledge have been made by Cichorius in two important works, by Schmitt in his treatment of the fragments of Books XXVI–XXX, and by Fiske in his *Lucilius and Horace*. Recently too an Italian scholar, Terzaghi, has published an edition of the text which noticeably departs from Marx's order, and a supplementary volume entitled *Lucilio*. In the latter he deals with Lucilius' times and, while disclaiming any notion of replacing Marx and Cichorius, gives particular attention to the extant pieces of Books XXVI–XXX and of the first three books, with an aim at connecting as many fragments as possible into a reasonable semblance of unity. In the preface to his larger book, one of four hundred and fifty pages, Terzaghi makes the significant remark that he would feel rewarded if only a tenth of the numerous pages which follow could be considered as containing something solid and sure (*qualcosa di sicuro*). This illustrates at once the attraction and the danger of work on Lucilius. The attempts to restore broken lines and to link fragment with fragment is in large part a subjective method according to which editors proffer for the same line different explanations, restore gaps differently, and imagine quite different contexts. The marvel then is that we have as much certainty as has been attained. Fortunately, the book is often specified along with a quotation by an ancient scholar: only to Books XXI and XXIV are no fragments referred on the evidence of antiquity.

The order of the thirty books is that of a posthumous edition: it is not that of composition, but follows a conventional arrangement which placed hexameter poems before elegiacs and elegiacs before iambics. The whole chronology presents difficulties. It is, however, usually agreed that the earliest group is XXVI–XXX. Book XXVI in all likelihood was the first of Lucilius' books to be published, as it contains lines which read as if they belonged to a prefatory treatment of satire. These five books appeared in a collected issue by the author in 123 B.C. Later came XXII–XXV and the latest books written were I–XXI, which were, like XXX, entirely in hexameters.

The scale of this course of lectures does not permit a survey of the books in detail; but some idea of the variety of theme may be conveyed. Book XXVI is chronologically in the forefront; logically, too, it deserves mention first, because of its prefatory character. It is, besides, important for the glimpses afforded into the Lucilian attitude to satire. Cichorius was the first to show that these fragments belong to an introduction (εἰσαγωγή) addressed to a young writer, Junius Congus, urging him to undertake an epic on contemporary exploits:

Blazon forth Popilius' battle, sing the lay of Scipio's deeds.

(*Pércrepa pugnám Popili, fácta Cornelí cane.*)

(Marx 621)

Lucilius for himself declares such composition to be foreign to his genius (Marx 622). His forte is satire, and he regards his poems as the spontaneous utterance of a natural impulse (*ex praecordiis, 590*). Simple language in the plain style which was favored in Stoic theory should enable him to appeal not to learned readers but to the ordinary man (595). So he ridicules the grand manner of tragedy (587) and Pacuvius' bombastic words (597, 599, 601, 602, 605). The satiric impulse must have its outlet somehow (*evadat saltem aliquid aliqua*, 632), after the impromptu fashion of the Stoico-Cynic διατριβή, which did not lay claim to be finished expression. But frank criticism would be welcomed from a true friend (611), whose honesty might be contrasted with the hypocritical grief of women hired to weep in a funeral procession:

> Female mourners paid in money for their tears at funerals
> Outdo others in hair-rending and their strident caterwauls.

> ([*út*] *mercede quaé conductae flént alieno in fúnere*
> *praéficae, multo ét capillos scíndunt et clamánt magis.*)

(954-955)

Literary discussion is present in several of the books of the same group; for example, XXVII, where he advocates the Stoic theory on relating style to facts as an essential for clear thinking. The author returns to the subject of satire in XXX, where he apparently introduces an adversary to twit him with the bitterness of his satire, which is alleged to assail and blame without accomplishing anything. But other literary themes occupied Lucilius. In Book V, where he uses epistolary form to remonstrate with a friend who did not visit him when he was ill, he humorously introduces words ending in a jingle—*nolueris, debueris*, the Isocratean ὁμοιοτέλευτα—and gives illustrations of alliteration. Book IX brings in critical and grammatical points, including the distinction between *poema* as a short poem and *poesis* as a long sustained poem like the *Iliad* or Ennius' *Annales*—probably in opposition to definitions by the poet Accius in his *Didascalica*. In that book he also touches on orthography, advocating the spelling of -*ei* for the nominative plural and -*i* for the genitive singular in what we call the second declension. The next book contains attacks on various literary personages, and its concern with style inspires Persius' opening satire. Book

XII introduces points in the history of tragedy. Here and
there in his works Roman poets came under the whip. We
know from Horace that he found faults in Ennius; his dis-
taste for tragic inflation led to his parodying the diction of
Pacuvius; and there are hits, open and suspected, at Accius,
his contemporary.

Philosophy and morality played a great part in his work.
Book IV assailed luxury and was the basis of Persius' third
satire. Book XV stigmatized various moral weaknesses—
superstition, avarice, and anger. It is here that he pours contempt on the groundless terror felt for hobgoblins invented
in the primitive times of "the Fauns and Numa Pompilius,"

> Like infants who mistake for living men
> Bronze statues, so they take imagined dreams
> For true, believing bronze has heart within.

> *(sic isti somnia ficta*
> *vera putant, credunt signis cor inesse in aenis.)*
>
> (Marx 486-488)

The meaninglessness of external possessions, if in excess, is
among the themes of XVIII, and the next book, XIX, on discontent with one's lot (the μεμψιμοιρία of the Greeks), treated
of a subject which enters into the first satire of Horace's
first book.[19] Book XXIX handled theories of life and the
teaching of morality as well as the Socratic view of friendship; but the preceding book, XXVIII, shows that Lucilius
did not always wear too grave a face, but could make fun of
Stoic pretensions to universal ability on the assumption that
the sage could be a Jack-of-all-trades, or, as he expresses it,

> Unsurpassable as tailor, cleverest to sow a patch.

> *(sárcinatorem ésse summum, súere centorem óptume.)*
>
> (747)

The same notion reappears in Horace's question: "If the wise
man is rich and a good cobbler and if he alone is handsome
and a king, why crave what you have got?"[20] Avarice is pre-

sumably "the dropsy of the mind" in this book (764) and anticipates the *dirus hydrops* of Horace's *Odes*. Elsewhere Lucilius makes a facetious use of the doctrine of the four elements, fire and water, earth and air, the first two of which are taken away from an offender by outlawry (the legal interdiction *aqua et igni*) and the remaining two, the earthy body and the breath of life, by capital execution. The sexual relations touched upon in Books VIII and XXIX influenced Horace's early study of the question in Satire I. ii, and the woman of easy virtue appears in VII and in one part of XXVII. "Collyra," the title of XVI according to Porphyrio, and "Hymnis," named several times in XXIX, bear testimony to Lucilius' own love affairs.

The moral dangers of luxury were doubtless fully exemplified in the dinner party of XIII and Granius' banquet in XX, which handed on the theme treated by Matron and other Greeks to the *cenae* of Horace's Nasidienus and Petronius' Trimalchio.[21] Public scandals incensed Lucilius. He flagellates commanders incompetent in the field and dishonesty of public life, where chicanery ruled, he declares, "from morning to night, on holiday and workday, among all ranks, commons and patricians alike, as might be seen in the forum, everyone bent on the same devices, to cheat if it could be done safely (*verba dare ut caute possint*), to beat an opponent by craft (*pugnare dolose*), to vie with others in flattery, to assume a mask of virtuous airs (*bonum simulare virum se*), and lay traps for others, as if every man were every man's enemy"—a stinging indictment from a critical observer. But if he could thus slash the city (to translate Persius' phrase),[22] he had also the gift of affection. His reverence for "great Scipio" (*Scipiadae magno*), as he calls him, and "our Scipio" is visible even in surviving scraps,[23] and a kindly note animates his memorial epigram on a slave in Book XXII:

> Here lies Metrophanes, a loyal slave
> And good, the pillar of Lucilius' house.

There is something particularly provoking in remembering how much of entertaining anecdote and of personal experience, almost "Confessions," we have lost through the gaps in Lucilius' works. One feature in him which especially charmed Horace was (to adapt a phrase by Whittier) his opening to the day the windows of his soul: "He in times gone by," says Horace,[24] "would confide his deepmost thoughts to his writings, as it were to trusty comrades; to no other quarter did he turn, whether things went ill with him or well: hence it comes that the old poet's whole life lies open to view, as if painted on a votive tablet"—words among which, in the Latin, we recognize the felicitous motto prefixed to Boswell's *Life* of Dr. Johnson. Thus, among anecdotes were those of the journey to the Sicilian straits through Capua (Bk. III), and of the bore who inflicted himself on the author—or was it on Scipio? (Bk. VI). Part of XIV introduced Scipio recounting his journey in the East, 140–138 B.C.; and, according to Cichorius,[25] Book XI contained a set of brief anecdotes, like the Greek χρεῖαι, concerning well-known contemporaries of the Scipionic Circle. One of these detailed the taunt addressed by the appropriately named Asellus to "great Scipio" himself. Personal confidences were likely to have been exemplified in the record of his amours already mentioned with his beloved Collyra and another inamorata, Hymnis. Nor was the burlesque tale lacking in Lucilius' repertory: in XVII there was a Cynic treatment, or rather maltreatment, of the story of Ulysses and his faithful Penelope, with a flippant parody on Homeric material.

In this brief survey of different books I have left to the end the first two. They may be fittingly mentioned here, as both are anecdotal in scheme. Book I represents, after the fashion of a Homeric parody, a conclave of the gods in which there is a mock-serious deliberation on whether Rome or the unjust judge Lupus is to perish—one or other would have to go under. There must have been real fun in this now tantalizingly mutilated conference. Apollo doesn't like to be called *pulcher* (the adjective might mean "pretty," but it had some not overpretty associations); Neptune apologizes for his absence from an earlier council, presumably because he had been away among "the blameless Ethiopians"; Jupiter is not allowed to forget his intrigues with Leda and with Dia, the wife of Ixion; and one of the retorts in the celestial debate is to the effect that the opposition is finding difficulties where none exist—"you're mad to search a bulrush for a knot"(the familiar Latin proverb *nodum in scirpo quaerere*). Book II contained a trial scene in which Q. Mucius Scaevola was prosecuted by T. Albucius for peculation in the province of Asia. To a slight degree it is a parallel to the wrangle in Horace, Satire I. vii, between two litigants, P. Rupilius Rex, of Praeneste, and the Greek Persius, before the judgment seat of Brutus; but Professor Fiske, who generally sees more borrowings from Lucilius in Horace than I do,[26] admits that here "no explicit verbal imitation is to be anticipated." The truth is that Horace's sketch is in large part a reminiscence of his own campaigning days, and his memory for an incident in his past experience may be supposed to be at least equal to his memory for Lucilius' writings. In Lucilius' trial scene the one litigant no doubt aimed at outdoing the other in abuse as much as in sound argument. The author would personally prefer the direct Latin style of Scaevola to the elaborate diction of Albucius, which, with its Greek insertions, is likened to a mosaic pavement of wriggly pattern. He intentionally employs the Greek word λέξεις to suggest a kind of *melange de phrases*, because Albucius was a Helleno-maniac to whom might be applied Butler's lines in Hudibras:[27]

> Beside, 'tis known he could speak Greek
> As naturally as pigs squeak.

This gives point to Scaevola's story in court, how, as a Roman praetor, he once met Albucius at Athens[28] and, instead

of giving him a Latin salutation, hailed him with "χαῖρε
Tite," as we might say "Bon jour, Monsieur Tite." He mischievously prompted his whole retinue to deluge him with
exactly the same words. The joke was too much for Titus'
liking: as Scaevola remarks, "thereby hangs the tale of Albucius' animosity to me" (*hinc hostis mi Albucius, hinc ini-
micus*). It is clear that this episode, like much in Lucilius,
came from no bookish source, but from an actual occurrence.

Lucilius is an honest satirist. Though he pillories others,
he does not pretend to be better than he is or better than
those whom he censures: *de se loquitur non ut maiore reprensis,*
Horace tells us in I. x. 55. He owns to having faults of his
own; and a greater number of continuous fragments might
have revealed more fully that inner personality which he
took no pains to conceal. As it is, the first person in the fragments, where we can be sure it is not from a dialogue, may
be taken to speak for the author himself.

His artistic attitude is a parallel to his equilibrium in philosophy. He could not fail to be drawn to comedy for its
realism; but it was the realism of Roman life around him
that produced his vivacious variety in theme. He holds the
mirror up to it in his recollections of the past and in his pictures of the men and morals of the day. He could turn the
literary epistle into a kind of open letter to the public, just as
at other times he could dip into learned problems, or, again
elsewhere, indulge his fantasy in burlesque. Amid a rising
flood of corruption, increasing uncertainty of life, and a men-
acing abandonment of much that might be treasured as a
sacred heritage of tradition, his voice was raised in sanity,
and often with the saving grace of humor, to serve his generation. His accents of warning came all the better from a
thinker to whom the blend of Academic with Stoic elements
gave a breadth of view that saved him from pedantry and
left him free to laugh at philosophers themselves, if extreme
in their doctrine. This lighter side in him explains, rather

than is explained by, his interest in the comedy of the past, both Greek and Latin. It was a deeper interest than is indicated merely by his verbal imitations[29] of Aristophanes and Plautus and Terence: it had a kinship with the spirit of the mime, with the διατριβή, and with the scoffing Menippus.

Lucilius is not to be termed a stylist. Indeed in his period Latin style was as yet imperfectly formed, as is evident from a comparison of Ennius, Pacuvius, and Accius with their unsurpassable Greek models in tragedy. All the less could finished style be expected in a satirist the nature of whose writing linked it confessedly with the common speech (*sermo cotidianus*)[30]—direct and vigorous, but in phrasing disjointed and unpolished. Yet Lucilius made his own contribution to Latin literature by examining principles of style and by practicing a plain manner of utterance. A mild tmesis of his like *conque tubernalem* (1137), for *contubernalemque*, does not justify the sneer of Ausonius[31] in the fourth century that a writer has only to practice such cutting up of words in order to copy Lucilius:

> You'll learn to split a proper name by tmesis:
> That will be true Lucilian mimesis.

> (*rescisso disces componere nomine versus,*
> *Lucili vatis sic imitator eris.*)

Clumsy his old hexameters may sound; they are, however, not often so badly constructed as is 1076 *pulmentaria, ut intubus aut aliquae id genus herba*; and they did in fact, by virtue of example, ordain for Roman satire its regular verse. His rhetorical training enabled him, when he chose, to invent an alliteration[32] or to parody bombast; and from his genius sprang the force which won him enthusiastic readers well into the imperial period. Allusion has been made to admirers of his in Tacitus' times. The question may be raised[33] whether, when Nonius quotes him as he so often does, he actually, as Marx believes,[34] possessed the old republican's writings still

complete, from which his secretarial slaves might make ex-
cerpts, or whether he drew at second hand from abridgments
based on the original. Birt[35] holds that Lucilius was still so
much in vogue about 400 A.D. that Claudian read and copied
from him direct. "Force is life," Lucilius says in one of his
lines, "the compelling force in all we do" (*vis est vita, vides,
vis nos facere omnia cogit*, 1340). This vigor and a wonderful
variety are among the intrinsic merits which outweigh his
negligent workmanship and formal defects.[36]

The literary obligations of Horace to Lucilius have been
much discussed since Iltgen published his *De Horatio Lucilii
Aemulo* in 1872. In 1876, writing in *Hermathena*, Professor
Tyrrell declared that the debt "is very much greater than is
generally supposed," and he returned to the subject later in
his *Lectures on Latin Poetry*. Since then, so full a study of
the matter has been made in Professor Fiske's *Lucilius and
Horace* that a brief consideration will suffice here. A remark
may be premised about borrowing or imitation, especially in
Classical literature. It does not necessarily spell unoriginal-
ity; everything depends on how the borrowing is done. Greek
sources do not make Latin literature second-hand any more
than the use of Italian *novelle* or of North's *Plutarch* makes
Shakespeare a plagiarist. Horace himself recognized the difference between free adaptation and slavish copying. In one
of his *Epistles*[37] he transmits through Julius Florus a warning to Celsus about the danger of pillaging the Palatine Library and decking himself in borrowed plumes. When Horace
took from Lucilius a story or situation, he not merely mo-
dernized it as Pope in the eighteenth century did with some
of Chaucer's tales of the fourteenth, but he also transformed
it by relating it to his own times and by adding his own experiences. Hints were got from Lucilius' journey to the Sicilian straits; some details, even unsavory details,[38] are re-
tained; others, like repeated and prosaic records of mileage,
are wisely dropped; but the whole result is a vivid diary of

travel to the Brindisi of Augustan times in which the two
great poets of the day, Virgil and Horace, are companions,
one—such is the realistic tone—in trouble with his digestion,
the other with his eyes. Further, in addition to the reconstruction of a whole narrative and the insertion of novel material, there was the stylistic improvement of a Lucilian
sketch. It was now refurbished in language and meter to suit
the more refined literary standard of the Augustan age.

The imitation takes two main forms: there is direct imitation of lines or phrases in Lucilius, as well as borrowing of
proper names,[39] and, secondly, there is adaptation of the idea
of some of his *Saturae*. The verbal imitations are numerous;
Porphyrion draws attention to many of them; and it is noticeable that they are spread over works composed by Horace
at different dates. The influence of Lucilius upon him was
therefore a lasting one. A few examples will illustrate this
point. In Satire I. v. 87 the name of a town is said to be
omitted as being metrically impossible in the hexameter,
mansuri oppidulo quod versu dicere non est (to stay in a little
town which can't be named in my verse): this conveys in
similar words the same sense as Lucilius 228-229, *quem plane
hexametro versu non dicere possis*, though the context is different. The saddlebag or *mantica* that galls the bobtailed
mule in Satire I. vi. 106 was taken, says Porphyrion, from a
Lucilian line, *ex Luciliano illo, mantica cantheri costas gravi-
tate premebat*. Later in the first book, at I. x. 30, *Canusini
bilinguis* echoes the *Bruttace bilingui* (1124) of Lucilius;[40]
and in the second book, at II. viii. 11, the picture of the high-
girt slave using a purple napkin to wipe the table almost repeats Lucilius 568, *purpureo tersit tunc latas gausape mensas*.
Even in the *Odes*, where the more elevated style was less
likely to admit satiric influence, the "dread dropsy" (*dirus
hydrops*) of the mind contains a Lucilian reminiscence, and
in the *Ars Poetica*, the passage on the overacted grief of
mourners is based on Lucilius, as already mentioned.[41]

There are similar borrowings in Varro, though it was Menippus rather than Lucilius who was Varro's real precursor. Varro repeats a Lucilian hexameter about eatables[42] and, like Lucilius in his ninth book, he draws a distinction between *poema* and *poesis*.

But Horace's imitation of Lucilius took also the form of imitation of subject-matter or adoption of a theme, as in the story of the journey to Brundisium and the encounter with the bore, where the narratives are entirely recast and the total result is typically Augustan and Horatian. In his dramatic picture of the bore—and Horace would have been lucky if he had not met specimens to study quite apart from Lucilius—the author, who begins with a Lucilian echo in *ibam forte*, gives us a sly acknowledgment of his debt, such as it was, at the very end of the ninth satire. "Him did Apollo snatch away," τὸν δ' ἐξήρπαξεν 'Απόλλων, says Lucilius, quoting Homer in the original Greek. Horace makes two changes. Since he has told the story inimitably as a personal experience, he changes the grammatical object to the first person singular, and, with his dislike for interlarding his work with Greek, he translates into Latin: *sic me servavit Apollo* —"that was the way Apollo rescued me from his clutches." It is noteworthy that Persius, who based two of his satires, the first and the third, on *saturae* by Lucilius, gives his own cue by a quotation from Lucilius in his opening line, "Oh, the worries of men! how empty is the world!" *O curas hominum! o quantum est in rebus inane!* It may be added that Horace's fourteenth Epistle, on country life, contains echoes of Lucilius, which led Tyrrell to regard this imaginary letter to Horace's farm steward as a clever restoration of Lucilius meant to be read by the entourage of Augustus.

There was much to commend Lucilius to Horace. His frank autobiographic jottings made their appeal. The two poets were akin in their preference for leisure over official duties. Lucilius would not change with a prosperous tax collector in Asia: Horace could politely but firmly decline an imperial secretaryship. In his anti-Caesarian days Horace would have been Pompeian enough to be attracted to the works of Lucilius, who was Pompey's grand uncle. Yet there was also much to repel Horace's fastidious taste. Lucilius, who had to struggle with an imperfectly developed Latin, was rough and hasty in composition—two great faults in Horace's eyes —and he was too fierce in his onslaughts. So, by the time Horace came to write the fourth and tenth satires of his first book, he was heartily tired of the undiscerning laudation of Lucilius by an over-enthusiastic set of critics. For them Horace, speaking on behalf of a period when style was worshiped as it was afterward in the Italian Renascence, felt that the best literary lesson must be the inculcation of rigid rules of Augustan taste and careful workmanship. It was not unnatural, then, that he should borrow hints from an old favorite (and he never withdrew from Lucilius a generous meed of respect and praise); nor was it out of place for him to show how his own personal experience and his literary powers enabled him to produce parallel works of far more finished art. Hence the metamorphosis of the Sicilian journey into Horace's own journey to Brundisium, and the transformation of the victim of Lucilius' impudent bore into Horace himself on the Via Sacra. Following the ancient practice of imitation, Horace found themes in Lucilius, as Lucilius had found themes in popular philosophic dialogues.[43] He is confessedly his follower—*sequor hunc*, he declares,[44] and, despite his many strictures upon his predecessor, he avows himself inferior to him as the true inventor of satire.[45]

What Quintilian likes in Lucilius is a quartette of qualities which he specifies—learning, frankness, sharpness of invective, wit, *nam eruditio in eo mira et libertas atque inde acerbitas et abundantia salis.*[46] Horace's attitude is, as we should expect, more complex. It is fully expressed in several passages[47] of his three *sermones* which deal particularly with the subject of satire, iv and x in Book I and i in Book II. I propose to conclude this study of Lucilius by giving the gist of Horace's words without comment, as their meaning will be clear from what has gone before and some of them have necessarily been cited already. Than this brief concluding paraphrase there can be no better introduction to Horace himself.

The gist of these passages in order is: (*Sat.* I. iv) Lucilius followed the Old Comedy of Greece as represented by Eupolis, Cratinus, and Aristophanes, in attacking the infamous, but he changed the meter. Lucilius is not wholly inelegant; he is shrewd but harsh in composition, and too fast. It suggests an author writing against time, two hundred verses per hour standing on one foot! No wonder that he flowed on like a muddy stream. He lacked self-criticism. "Satire, such as mine or that of Lucilius," remarks Horace, "has a prose element: remove the meter and it is *sermo pedester*. It is not meant to be poetic in diction." Then, in Satire X, in reply to criticisms on the foregoing, he retorts: "Why, yes, I did say that Lucilius' lines run on with halting foot. But surely Lucilius' verses are acknowledged to be rough. Admittedly he rubbed the city smartly down with Attic salt. That doesn't make a poem, however. Lucilius was too fond of a medley of Greek and Latin words. Isn't Latin good enough?" asks Horace. "To write Greek nowadays is to carry wood into the forest." Horace had long outgrown his early compositions in Greek verse. He says he writes better satire than Varro of Atax, who was a failure in his attempts (*experto frustra*); but he acknowledges he is not the equal of the inventor of satire. What though he criticized Lucilius! This does not mean that he would venture to pluck from his brow his wreath of fame:

> *neque ego illi detrahere ausim*
> *haerentem capiti cum multa laude coronam.*

"Is no fault to be found in Homer? Didn't Lucilius himself pass adverse comments on Ennius? It is a fair question, in reading Lucilius, to ask ourselves whether he or his subject was to blame for his want of polish and melody. If only he had belonged to our Augustan age, he would prune with care."

In Satire II. i, the lawyer Trebatius advises Horace to celebrate Caesar's exploits, as Lucilius did Scipio's. Horace replies that his forte is satire—nothing so ambitious as epic poetry. In writing satire he is best pleased to model himself upon Lucilius, the fine old poet who revealed his inner life to his books, where it may be read as in a picture. But, it may be asked, isn't satire dangerous? Well, Lucilius didn't find it so: he led the way in unmasking shams—fair-seeming shams. Did he thereby offend his great friends, Laelius and Scipio? No, he was the friend of Virtue and of Virtue's friends: and this moral force did not prevent him from quietly enjoying the pleasures of society. His example has been of value; for Horace, also, though he owns himself Lucilius' inferior both in station and in genius, has learned the lesson of living with the great.

The final impression left is that, while Horace was well aware of Lucilius' defects, he paid him the sincerest flattery of imitation and entertained for him genuine admiration and respect.

CHAPTER IV

HORACE

Ridentem dicere verum
quid vetat?
HORACE *Sat.* I. i. 24-25
Omne vafer vitium ridenti Flaccus amico
tangit et admissus circum praecordia ludit
PERSIUS I. 116-117

No ONE writing upon Horace is likely—least of all about the time of his bimillenary—to be "gravelled for lack of matter." The quandary is rather how to escape embarrassment from the riches in the Horatian scholarship of past centuries. Long before any printed *editio princeps*, there had accumulated a considerable store of learning from the ancient *scholia*, and since printing began there has been a galaxy of famous editors and commentators. It may be enough merely to recall a few such outstanding figures as Lambin, Cruquius (Cruuke), Bentley, Orelli, Keller and Holder, and Wickham. Students of the *Satires* in particular must all feel their debt to Cartault's *Étude* and to the editions of Palmer, Lejay, Kiessling and Heinze, and in America to those by Rolfe, Greenough, Morris, and Fairclough.

Horace is the greatest and most versatile of Roman satirists—greatest, because he remains unrivaled in that restrained economy of power which genius bestowed upon him, and most versatile, because no Roman satirist equaled him in his almost infinite variety. He proved, too, that satire could be potent and incisive without reliance upon indignation and venom. The truth, even an unpalatable one, can be told with a smile.

There is another point worth emphasis in a survey of his works. From first to last the satiric was never entirely absent from his writings. Present in the majority of the *Epodes*, it appears at times even among his lyrics, where the prevailing inspiration, which has charmed readers century after cen-

tury, has also amply justified his own claim to be at his most
poetic height, and where, in general, he departed farthest
from themes and diction which were more nearly allied to
conversation (*sermoni propiora*). Later in his career, after he
had in his own view said goodbye to true poetry and had
found a new means of expression in the verse epistle, he
again and again returned to the satiric note, human in its
interest, and humane in utterance. Satire is not primarily to
be looked for to any great degree in the specially literary
Epistles of Book II; but they are not without shrewd hits at
the absurd bigotry of admiring old poetry just because it is
old, at the awkwardness, too, of deciding exactly when an
author is old, and at the notion that anyone can be a poet,
for the mere trying—"Scholars and dunces, we write verse
galore" (*scribimus indocti doctique poemata passim*), an innocent scribbling craze that after all has its merits.[1] Again
he jests at the spectacular extravagance in historical pageant-
plays—what fun they would have been for the laughing philosopher, Democritus![2] It is also worth observing that the
Ars Poetica, or *Epistle to the Pisos*, both begins and ends in
ironic humor. At its opening, Horace satirizes the violation
of literary unity by imagining friends of his at a show of mon-
strously incongruous pictures such as a horse's neck joined
to a human head or a pretty woman tailing off into a fish—
"Would you be able to keep from laughing?" he asks. And
there is a facetious conclusion of the poem to match.[3] It is a
satire on spurious inspiration. The mad poet is a person to
whom wise folk give a wide berth—urchins hoot at him as a
figure of fun. Head in air, he belches out his lines. Like a
bird-catcher intent on the flying game, he goes flop into a well
or a pit, but although he yells "Help, help!" there's nobody
to pull him out. No wonder! for how do you know he didn't
do it intentionally? Didn't Empedocles jump into the crater
of Aetna to get an immortal halo? Poets surely must have
the privilege of perishing!

> To rescue anyone against his will
> Is just as bad as an attempt to kill.
>
> (*invitum qui servat idem facit occidenti.*)

Even if dragged out, he won't be reasonable. His boring recitations drive everybody off the scene. If he catches anyone he holds him fast (like Coleridge's ancient mariner), and does him to death by reading his poems, like a leech that won't let the skin go until it is gorged with blood. In such an ironic close to a serious poem we have the traditional "jocular-earnest" of τὸ σπουδαιογέλοιον revived.

This affords a reason why it is impossible to omit the *Epistles* in an estimate of Horace as a satirist. It is still convenient to retain the old titles of *Satirae* and *Epistulae*; but without discussing the question of Horace's own title for these divisions of his work, one must remember that he himself described both as *sermones*, and that in many the themes handled are akin.[4]

Horace was born at Venusia in South Italy in 65 B.C., and died at Rome in 8 B.C. His father, an ex-slave, tax collector, and owner of a small farm, was able to secure for his boy an excellent education. Five years younger than Virgil, Horace was over twenty when Julius Caesar was murdered in 44 B.C. He was then a student of Greek literature and philosophy at Athens, and with anti-Caesarian enthusiasm he served under Brutus in the East until the rout of Philippi cut short his career as officer in the republican army.

He had not taken the right side for worldly prospects. On his return to Rome, finding the paternal property confiscated, he had the scantiest of means. Work as a quaestor's clerk kept him from starvation; disillusion for a time drove him into reckless living; only his verse remained as a pursuit worthy of his education and talent. It gradually attracted notice and in 38 B.C. he had been introduced by his poet friends Virgil and Varius to Maecenas, the statesman whose

generous patronage of literature made his name a proverb.
This brought him into touch with Octavian Caesar,"Augustus" that was to be. Maecenas' gift to him in 33 B.C. of a farm
among the Sabine hills ensured him a competency and a retreat for thought and writing. By degrees Horace realized
that Rome's future depended on the stable government promised by Caesar's grandnephew. His detestation of Antony's
dangerous Oriental schemes found clear expression in his
notes of triumph over Octavian's victory at Actium in 31
B.C., and thenceforward he was a wholehearted supporter
of the new regime as the firmest guaranty for the peace and
morality of Rome.

For our present purpose his career can best be traced by
glancing at his works in order. They are the *Satires*, Book I,
35 B.C.; *Satires*, Book II (like the preceding book, in hexameters), 30 B.C.; *Epodes*, or "iambi," in the same year; the
Odes, or "carmina,"in varied meters following Greek models,
of which the first three books were issued together in 23 B.C.
and which, though not without satiric pieces, do not so closely
concern us here; his other lyrics, the *Carmen Saeculare*, in
celebration of the games organized by Augustus in 17 B.C.,
and the fourth book of the *Odes* in 13 B.C. But before 13, before his return to lyric, Horace had issued in hexameter verse
many of his maturest reflections upon life in the first book of
the *Epistles*, 20 or 19 B.C. The second book shows that he has
turned more completely from the study of his social environment to the study of the principles of literature. It consists
of two elaborate hexameter letters. Letter i, mainly on drama
and aspects of early Latin literature, belongs to 13 B.C. or
possibly 12; and ii, mainly on style, may be the older of the
two poems: there is, however, a wide range in the dates proposed for it—19 or 12 or even 10 B.C. This concentration on
literary themes does not wholly break with tradition in satire, if Lucilian example is remembered; but in style the gulf
between Horace and his predecessor is immeasurable.

The one remaining work is the *Ars Poetica*, as generations have called it, or the *Epistula ad Pisones*. Its date has been much canvassed. Some have considered it Horace's last work: it may, however, have come out, after the *Carmen Saeculare*, in 17 or 16 B.C., though recently Immisch has argued for an earlier date, 20 or 19 B.C., and still more recently an attempt has been made to push it back to 28-27.[5] It does not offer an exhaustive handling of poetry, because its interest and themes are limited by Horace's hopes for a resuscitation of Roman drama. With Horatian additions, Horatian examples, and Horatian common sense, it is a free adaptation of literary precepts originally laid down by Neoptolemus of Parium and passed on by Philodemus as an intermediary.[6]

In Book I of the *Satires* some of Horace's earliest work was comparatively crude. His apprentice-like studies were rather too much after the manner of Lucilius. The oldest of all is vii, a reminiscence of a squabble between a pair of rapscallions before Brutus' tribunal in Asia Minor. Such scolding matches were recurrent sources of amusement from Lucilius onward. In his account of the journey to Brundisium, Horace makes a mock-epic digression of twenty lines to narrate how he and his fellow travelers enjoyed a merry time at supper listening to the abusive repartees between Sarmentus the jester and Messius Cicirrus the Oscan.[7] How persistent this altercation motif was, and how true to the Italian character, may be illustrated in one of Marcus Aurelius' letters which relates that, at the close of a busy day of work in the country, the family took supper in the oil-press room and were enlivened with the diversion of hearing peasants chaff each other. Another early satire is the second, concerned with the satisfaction of sexual appetite, and Lucilian in its coarseness. The eighth, also early, though without traces of Lucilian influence, is a jocular tale of the fright which a statue of the garden-god Priapus gave to the witches Canidia and Sagana. The other satires of the book were written between

38 and 35 B.C., that is, after Horace had become acquainted
with Maecenas. Of these the two anecdotic sketches, v and
ix, owe, as previously indicated, something to Lucilius, but
are, notwithstanding, personal experiences of Horace. It is
perhaps because he keeps so strictly to his own experiences
in the diary of his journey that he misses the chance of giving fuller details of interest about his fellow travelers in the
fifth satire. In any event, he is incomparably more skillful
and vivid in describing his encounter on the Via Sacra with
the insupportable bore on whose impenetrable encasement
of self-sufficiency Horace's ironic politeness is entirely thrown
away. For the reader every stroke of its clever dialogue tells.
It is a dramatic sketch[8] in three scenes—the first, where
nothing that Horace says can keep his unwelcome companion from thrusting himself upon the poet or from thinking
that bribery and push will win access to Maecenas; the second scene, where his friend Aristius Fuscus mischievously
avoids rescuing Horace; the third, where an unexpected re-
lease is effected by the appearance of the plaintiff in a law
suit in which the bore had been summoned to show cause.
Satire iii, adroitly placed next to Satire ii, with which its
kindly tone is in sharp contrast, delivers a homily on the
uncharitableness of men's judgments and a plea for mutual
forbearance in the name of the true friendship valued by
Epicureans as an essential for happiness. It is, therefore, in
keeping with the spirit of iv and x, where, as already shown,
Horace answers criticisms on his poetry from devotees of the
Lucilian school of satire, negatively, by disclaiming his right
to be called a poet at all in virtue of writing satire, and, positively, by proclaiming his own more excellent way of eschew-
ing rancor. "That is a blemish which I promise, if I can
honestly promise anything, shall be absent from my pages."
Nevertheless, he craves pardon for an occasional frankness
in reproof; for it had been his father's system to combine
theoretical admonition with practical examples of moral fail-

ure. So Horace will apply the same method in his own case
by taking himself to task in moments of quiet reflection. Has
he not one small fault—the satirist's peccadillo of amusing
himself on paper in moments of leisure? For such trifling he
ironically beseeches indulgence: "If you won't grant that
indulgence, there will come to reënforce me a mighty band
of 'poets' (here he slyly drops his previous pretense that he
was no poet); for we are far and away the majority and, like
the proselytizing Jews, we'll force you to join our throng." [9]
Satire x, as we have seen, continues Horace's answer to pro-
Lucilian enthusiasts, and the very fact of criticizing his
predecessor even in measured terms indicates a degree of
emancipation from his influence. Satire vi must always be
recognized as a fascinating autobiographic sketch of Horace,
the freedman's son, and of his debt to his father's guidance
as well as to his intimacy with Maecenas. In defending his
patron and the circle of friends to which the humbly born
author has been admitted, he touches on a subject which re-
curs in the *Epistles*, how to live with the great.

In the second book of the *Satires* Horace resorts more frequently to dialogue: it is used in six out of the eight, namely
in i, iii, iv, v, vii, and viii: ii is rather a monologue by Ofellus
on frugal fare, and vi, though dialogue is not its framework,
introduces dialogue between the Town Mouse and the Country Mouse. The dialogue form in most of these is noteworthy
in contrast with its inversion into letter form afterward in
the *Epistles*. In *Satires* II. ii, for example, Ofellus, as the poet's
old rustic friend who was a sage without rules (*abnormis sapiens*), lectures him on plain living (*nec meus est sermo sed
quae praecepit Ofellus*), and in the next satire Damasippus,
a recent convert to Stoicism, twits Horace with Epicurean
indolence. But, in the *Epistles*, it is Horace who delivers the
homilies, as he does to Lollius[10] on the Stoic view of the moral
value of Homer, or to Numicius[11] (whose obscure name appears to retain the epistolary form) on philosophic calm.

The opening words of the second book, *est quibus in satura videor nimis acer*, lead to an assertion of his right to speak as openly as Lucilius did, despite the libel laws at Rome. In the best kind of satire, he maintains, in accord with Lucilius' example,[12] personal criticism is subordinate to a salutary moral purpose. The next satire, already mentioned as a discourse on plain living by a yeoman of the old school, recommends hard work as giving the best appetite and declares that the costliest dishes must fail to satisfy those bloated by excess. With this satire should be read other two in the book, namely, iv and viii. All of them turn upon the culinary motif observed in Greek descriptions of a δεῖπνον and in Lucilius. But there is this difference. A grave tone characterizes Ofellus' precepts as contrasted with the humorous raillery of iv and viii. In iv Horace, jesting at some aspects of Epicureanism, ridicules in the person of Catius those connoisseurs in toothsome delicacies for whom the precepts of the happy life (*vitae praecepta beatae*) of the closing line were to be found not in philosophy but in cookery. The "precepts"[13] make a skit upon the rules of philosophers; the fun lies in the mockseriousness of Catius as he repeats his brief notes on a gastronomic lecture by a professor whose name, perhaps discreetly, he withholds; and the close, following a usual Horatian practice, is ironic. Feigning rapturous admiration for Catius' lore, Horace begs to be taken to a lecture given by the author of so much table wisdom, and he ends in words calculated by their Epicurean ring to parody Lucretius:[14] "*You* have been lucky enough to behold the sage's face and bearing, and you think little of that, because it just fell to your lot; but I feel an extraordinary passion to be able to approach the sequestered well-springs and quaff the rules for the happy life." In viii we find these very rules of the happy life being practiced at a dinner where Maecenas was a guest. Fundanius, the comic poet, tells Horace vivaciously how the party was given by Nasidienus Rufus. There is no proof that

Nasidienus was an actual name. Decorum indeed would rather suggest that it was fictitious; it would argue a shabby lapse in manners for a guest to make fun of hospitality which he had accepted. This raises the question of proper names in Horace.[15] Some of them, especially in Book I of the *Satires*, where he is more personal, were real: some were taken over from Lucilius; others were chosen to suggest character, like Pantolabus, "Grab-all," for a miser, or Porcius, the "Mr. Pigly" of this satire at whom the other guests laughed as he swallowed the cakes whole. It is a familiar device in literature, either in the obvious form of such names as Aristophanes' "Euelpides" (Goodhopeson), and Peithetairos (Winfriend), and Bunyan's "My Lord Time-Server" and "Mr. Facing-Both-Ways" or again in the slightly more disguised form of "Mrs. Proudie," the bishop's wife in Trollope, and "Sir Willoughby Patterne" in Meredith's *Egoist*. Whether Nasidienus was a real name or not, it signified an ostentatious parvenu of the type already emerging in the early empire. As Italian and Greek wines are being served, the host takes care to say he has other wines in his cellar. His vulgarity is brought out in his fussy exposition of the merits of everything put on the table, foreshadowing, as much else in him does, the still more elaborate study of Trimalchio by Petronius. But Nasidienus' ostentation, by poetic justice, culminated in a fiasco when a dust-laden tapestry collapsed on top of his precious viands. Then the ill-bred host bursts into angry tears over the accident instead of apologizing gracefully. He does, however, retire to the kitchen to restore the fortunes of his banquet. Talk goes on in the dining room until at last the host returns radiant (*mutatae frontis.*) But when he starts once more to spoil his dainties by tedious accounts of them, his guests leave him without so much as tasting his exhibits. It was just as if the witch Canidia had blown her poisonous breath on them!

Satires iii and vii handle two Stoic paradoxes: "all save

the sage are mad" and "all save the sage are slaves"; but while the former betrays Lucilian influence, there is little of it in vii, or in v, on legacy hunting, or in vi, on the idyllic peace of the country. In any event, Horace's relation to Lucilius had never been, even where closest, much more than might be described by the oxymoron "independent dependence."

The *Epodes* are not in the tradition of *satura*; but they are in large part, though not entirely, satiric; and they make up a medley of themes. The first epode, one of several addressed to Maecenas, is obviously not satiric in Horace's profession of readiness to go with his friend to the ends of the earth; nor is ix, in its proposal to celebrate the victory of Actium in wine; nor xiii, which is convivial after the fashion of Anacreon rather than of Archilochus; nor yet the two national Epodes, vii, on the horrors of civil war, and xvi, which expresses a pessimistic view of Rome's prospects. But the satiric note is very audible in Epode ii, the praises of country scenery by Alfius, the moneylender, who forgets its charms when there are loans to place; iii, to "merry Maecenas," an execration of garlic; iv, a lampoon on an ex-convict who had become a military officer and a landowner; vi, a defiance to a libeller, with a warning that Horace can bite back; viii and xii, grossly indecent in their abuse; and x, an inverted "send-off" poem (προπεμπτικόν), hoping that the poetaster Maevius might be lost at sea. Well within the range of topics usual in satire are xi, xiv, and xv, all three on personal experience in love. There is, besides, a pair of imaginary episodes—v, a mock-serious attempt to make the flesh creep by describing a boy victim in the power of four witches led by Canidia, and xvii (the finale of the miscellany), an ironic surrender by Horace to the same witch, who declares herself unrelenting. These last two recall the spirit of the mime; and for us the importance of the whole collection lies in the varied training which it gave to Horace in producing satiric effect.

Published about the same time as the second book of *Satires*, the *Epodes* contain more immature work; but in the first book of the *Epistles*, issued ten years later, about 20 or 19 B.C., the advance in ripeness of thought and expression is marked. Not only had Horace reflected deeply in the meantime, but his years of concentration on the *Odes*, published in 23 B.C., had brought him greater sureness and finish of literary touch to match his profounder criticisms upon society.

The first book of the *Epistles*, which as *sermones* claim our attention, shows that an ethical preoccupation now dominates Horace. In I. i, addressing Maecenas, he claims the right to retire from composing lyrics and to study philosophy as suited to his advancing years:

> Verse and all other trifles I resign:
> The true, the fitting are my sole concern.

> (*Versus et cetera ludicra pono:*
> *quid verum atque decens curo et rogo, et omnis in hoc sum.*)

Wisdom is the business of life, not the wasteful expenditure of human energy to avoid poverty and to act on the prevalent Roman slogan,

> Ho! Citizens, search first of all for cash!

> (*O cives, cives, quaerenda pecunia primum est!*)

It is here that he proclaims his independent eclecticism in the often quoted words,

> Not bound by oath to any master's words.

> (*nullius addictus iurare in verba magistri.*)

He is, therefore, a free lance who, though he values virtue as a social asset, can mock at the Stoic idea of the sage as a *rex:* why, boys can make a *rex* in their games,[16] he points out; and, as if anxious not to appear overserious, he resumes in an ironical close his jest at the supremacy of the Stoic sage:[17]

"To conclude: the Sage is inferior to Jove alone: he is rich, free, raised to honors, handsome—king of kings, in fine; preëminently hale and sound, save when troubled with a cold in the head."

More than half the poems in the book are less than fifty lines long, and broadly the shorter epistles seem more familiar, and the longer more formal. One pleasant feature is the peep at Horace as a literary counselor tendering almost paternal advice to young men who, like Julius Florus (I. iii), himself a satirist,[18] were serving on the staff of Tiberius, when sent to the East in 20 B.C. to put Tigranes on the throne of Armenia. Horace is interested in the literary plans of the young nobles in Tiberius' suite. He is also a philosophic monitor: to Celsus Albinovanus he writes (I. viii) in a tone of disillusion and self-reproach, perhaps as a hint to the youth that success has its dangers. To Tiberius himself he indites an *epistula commendaticia* (I. ix) on behalf of his friend Septimius.[19] In iv he pictures Albius (probably the elegiac poet Tibullus) as a man of leisure on his estate at Pedum, and in the same piece gives his own portrait with a dash of irony: "For myself, when you want a laugh, you'll find me plump, sleek, and in trim condition, a porker from Epicurus' herd." Yet such pretence did not make him an orthodox Epicurean. It is true that his invitation to the advocate Torquatus (I. v) to dine with him in honor of the Emperor's birthday is coupled with the praises of wine and talk. This may be called his occasional Epicureanism. But in writing to his farm bailiff (I. xiv), who restlessly yearns for the town when in the country, he preaches at him in the name of Stoic *constantia*, and the principles which pervade the epistolary homilies as a whole are Stoic principles.

A few more letters, however, of personal interest may be mentioned before glancing at those which are mainly homilies. He writes to Vinius about presenting Horatian poetry to Augustus at a suitably chosen moment, much as Martial

long afterward makes a request that his flippant and far from
puritanic epigrams must await the right time for presentation to the serious-minded younger Pliny.[20] There is a personal note, too, in Horace's plea to Maecenas that for
health's sake he must have independence of movement out
of and into Rome in I. vii, where he tells a good story about
the harm done by an interfering patron, and incidentally
records his own appearance in youth: "If you don't want
me ever to go away anywhere from Rome, you will have to
restore my strong lungs, and my black locks on a narrow
forehead; you will have to restore my pleasant prattle, restore my graceful laugh, and my lamentation at our wine
party when saucy Cinara ran away."[21] Epistles xvii and xviii
touch a subject of vast importance in Horace's life, the etiquette observable with patrons; but in both poems philosophic aspects of the question find a place. In xvii Horace
tells the story of Diogenes the Cynic, in the act of cleaning
vegetables for a meal, calling out to Aristippus the Cyrenaic
as he passed by, "If Aristippus could put up with dining on
greens, he would not want to associate with princes," to
which came the retort, "If my critic knew how to associate
with princes, he would turn up his nose at greens." The Horatian advice is to leave the snappish critic to his folly, and
to recognize the Cyrenaic as more adaptable to the circumstances of life. In xviii, to the discussion of making friends
among the great is fittingly appended the practical philosophy of making a friend of oneself.

In Epistle xix, written in scorn of criticasters, the personal
note is again prominent. Horace claims originality in lyric
and in *iambi*, but he declines to court notice for his poetic
trifles by giving public readings: in consequence he is thought
stand-offish and affected. His farewell to his book (I. xx) is
a delightful epilogue on what comes of being published. He
prophesies the fate awaiting his volume. Stammering age
will overtake it as it teaches boys their elements; yet the

reading-book can at least give information concerning the author and so he closes with an autobiographic vignette:

You will tell them that I was a freedman's son and, amid slender means, outstretched my wings too wide for the nest, so that you'll add to my merits as much as you take from my pedigree: you'll say that both in war and peace I found favour with the foremost men of Rome; describe me as short of stature, grey ere my time, fond of sunning myself, quick-tempered, yet readily appeased. If any one happen to ask you my age, let him learn that I completed four and forty Decembers in the year when Lollius called Lepidus his colleague [i.e., 21 B.C.].[22]

Stoicism colors more and more deeply his ethical epistles. In his letter to Lollius (I. ii), on the Stoic notion of the moral value of Homer, he preaches self-control betimes, and the crisp maxims present an affinity to the *sententiae* of the mime-writer Publilius Syrus in the Caesarian age.[23] Similarly the Stoic principle of "according to nature" is inherent in the eulogy of the simplicity and freedom of rural life which he addressed to his friend Aristius Fuscus, a literary man to whom Acron ascribed tragedies and Porphyrion comedies (I. x). It was he who played Horace the trick of leaving him in the clutches of the bore on the Via Sacra; and it was he whom he assured in the *Integer vitae* ode that the innocent heart needs no arms for its protection. To the philosophy of vi, the *Nil admirari* epistle, and of xvi, on the Stoic text that virtue is sufficient in itself for happiness, allusion will presently be made in considering the development of Horace's outlook upon life.

The keynote as well as the ultimate justification of satire is in its outlook upon life. Our survey has illustrated phases of Horace's attitude as a spectator and critic of his environment. It remains to summarize some aspects in the development of that attitude. Certain basic facts or factors contributory to his achievement, though of course they do not explain his genius, come out clearly from what has already been

said—his father's direction of his early life; his own study of
Greek literature and Greek philosophy both in Rome and in
Athens; his study of the older Latin poets and especially of
Lucilius; his own varied contact with men as student, as republican officer, as a ruined opponent of the new regime,
then as a welcome member of Maecenas' cultured circle for
thirty years, and as a convinced supporter of the young imperial system. Stress must in particular be laid upon this
intimacy with Maecenas, whose bounty secured him leisure
and placed him in such a position that he could observe contemporary society from the imperial court down to humble
slaves. Throughout he remained an interested spectator of
a period during which civil peace was regained and social
relations tranquilized. His earliest writings in the first book
of the *Satires*—a wonderful miscellany for a man of thirty
to publish—already show keen and fundamental understanding of his fellow men, though there was yet to come a deep-
ened philosophy of life and a mellower attitude to others.
In this evolution there are traceable a greatly lessened belief
in Epicureanism and a greatly increased belief in a reasonable Stoicism, a Stoicism cleared of its extravagances by a
sympathetic discernment of human limitations. It is symp-
tomatic, then, that in the first book of the *Satires* we should
find a preference for the Epicurean doctrine of society and
friendship expressed in a long passage based upon Lucretius,[24]
and also find elsewhere another Lucretian attitude adopted
toward the local wonder of melting incense at Egnatia on
the way to Brindisi: "The Jew Apella may believe it, not I:
the philosophy I have learned holds that the gods lead an
existence free from care, and that if nature works a miracle,
it is not the gods who in their gloom send it down from their
high home in heaven."

Questions are more fully argued out in the prevailing dia-
logue-form of *Satires*, Book II. The growing Stoic influence
colors Ofellus' panegyric on simple fare and the contrasted

picture of table luxury. There is a charming peep at a country meal when a visitor drops in to take potluck, or at least what could be prepared at once independently of the resources of a neighboring town. Then a piece of reflection closes the satire: "The land itself may be uncertain in tenure, one holder soon succeeding another"—from which the inference is in Stoic vein:

> So live with bravery,
> Pitting brave hearts against adversity,[25]

where he does not, as sometimes in the *Odes*, which had still to be published, argue in Epicurean manner from life's uncertainty and brevity, "Eat, drink; for tomorrow we die." Although in two satires[26] of the book he makes game of paradoxical Stoic tenets, it is with sympathetic gusto that in one of them he puts into Davus' mouth an excellent definition of moral freedom: "Who then is free? The wise man who holds sway over himself, undaunted by poverty or death or bonds, valiant to resist desire and to disdain high office, and in himself a sphere, complete and shaped and round, so that naught without has power to rest on that smooth surface— one on whom Fortune is crippled in her rush."[27]

The *Odes*, published seven years later, contain work of different stages in Horace's development. Much is occasional, transient, imaginary: as we should expect, some are in Epicurean, some in Stoic vein. The recipe for a chill winter day when Soracte stands deep in snow is pleasant company, the festal hour, and enjoyment while youth lasts—the doctrine of "Gather ye rosebuds while ye may"as summarized in the *Carpe diem* of another ode.[28] Yet any sensible Epicurean knew that wine was but a superficial prescription, and Horace recognized that there must be a limit in potations.[29] There is a significant invitation in III. xxix to Maecenas to share an unpretentious meal, leaving behind him "the reek, the wealth, and the din of Rome." Horace there claims in-

dependence of fickle Fortune through the restriction of desire—a thoroughly Stoic trait: "I wrap me in my native
worth; I seek for honest poverty with ne'er a dower."[30]

But nowhere is the growing hold of combined Platonism
and Stoicism more evident than in the six national odes which
open the third book. Horace has realized that he is both
"minstrel of the Roman lyre" (*Romanae fidicen lyrae*) and
"priest of the Muses" (*Musarum sacerdos*) whose mission is
directed to the youth of the land (*virginibus puerisque canto*).
On the moral health of the rising generation he knew must
depend the prosperity of Rome, and this realization is con-
current with a piety deeper, as he avows in I. xxxiv, than in
errant days when he was the votary of a wild philosophy
(*insanientis sapientiae*). No longer an infrequent and neglectful worshiper (*parcus deorum cultor et infrequens*), he can
now indite an ode on true religion to the peasant woman
whom he calls Phidyle,[31] and he has thus moved far away
from Epicurean skepticism.

There came, however, a time when Horace said what he
meant for his farewell to lyric and turned to those *sermones*
which we know as the *Epistles*. There is now a fuller accept-
ance of Stoic theory and less frequent ridicule of Stoic oddi-
ties. Yet Horace is careful to guard himself by his declaration
that he is pledged to the tenets of no one school. His Epicureanism was not mere levity and heedlessness, as his praise
of carefree revels might lead one to suppose. In his most
Epicurean days he had been an Epicurean with this difference, that he reflected, and so could not live entirely for the
pleasure of the passing moment. In any case, deeply in-
grained in him was his belief in moderation. His saying
"'Tis sweet to lose one's head upon occasion"(*dulce est de-
sipere in loco*)[32] is no counsel of reckless abandonment, and
his plea for "moderation in all things" (*est modus in rebus*)[33]
is a maxim which applies equally to his Epicureanism and
his Stoicism. No man ever valued more the golden mean; for

his *aurea mediocritas* offered a pledge of sovereign value for sanity, sobriety, safety in life, and he significantly uses the word *tutus* in his well-known passage in the *Odes*.[34] He hated therefore, not only the falsehood but also the danger of extremes. A professed eclectic, he took the teaching of the two rival philosophical schools with the qualification requisite for the avoidance of extremes, finding wisdom in both systems, as Seneca, a convinced Stoic, did when he quoted with approval Epicurean maxims in his earlier letters. And so with Stoicism: to Horace, while its paradoxes were absurd and impractical, its quietly dignified doctrines offered a salvation of the spirit. But a good deal of aversion and repugnance had first to be overcome. When scandalized by paradoxes, he prefers Epicurean common sense; nor could his shy dislike of the mob (*odi profanum vulgus et arceo*) or of popular Stoico-Cynic preaching to the mob do anything but prejudice him against parts of the system of the Porch. Yet gradually the time came when under the forbidding exterior of bigoted dogma and vulgar harangue he fully appreciated the greatness of the Stoic creed. Clearly, before the date of the *Epistles*, he is moved by the nobility of a true Stoic in drawing the Regulus of the *Odes*, or his *iustum et tenacem propositi virum*.[35] The Stoic emerges triumphant when the whole earth is vanquished save the relentless spirit of Cato:

> *cuncta terrarum subacta*
> *praeter atrocem animum Catonis.*[36]

This hold of Stoicism upon him was intensified by serious reflection during the period when Horace learned to love the country more deeply as his retreat in the hills gave him the repose of body and mind which made an ideal setting for Stoic "undisturbedness" (ἀταραξία).

It is this ἀταραξία of soul that he advocates in the first of the two epistles (I. vi) reserved as a conclusion to this study of Horace. Philosophic calm is the secret of bliss. Acting on this famous maxim of *nil admirari*, one should never lose one's head in excitement over anything. We are back to *est modus in rebus*. Virtue itself pursued to fanatical excess would not be in Horace's view the *summum bonum*. Tranquillity, the Stoic ἀπάθεια, is the ideal to be sought; for the ardent quest in society after riches, honors, luxury, love, and pleasure, defeats itself. Sometimes a blemish has been alleged against this epistle in that it seems inconsistently to break away into a totally different line of advice. This is to miss Horace's irony, which virtually implies, "If you disbelieve my theory, put energy into your own aims—'Queen Money can give birth and beauty!' "[37] It is as if he broke off to give the sarcastic advice, "By all means try *your* way instead of mine, and see where it leads"—*cultivez votre jardin*. Thinking also of a couplet in Mimnermus[38] which may be translated

> The Golden Goddess Love gives life its joy;
> Death take me when I quit dear Love's employ,

Horace concludes: "If, as Mimnermus holds, without love and gaiety naught is joyous, then live 'mid love and gaiety. Live long, farewell! If you know aught better than these counsels, be frank and share them: if not, join me in following these."

The irony here takes account of the Epicurean position as a kind of second best. But in the other Epistle which claims our notice, I. xvi, more exalted moral principles are inculcated. It is a disquisition upon the Stoic text that virtue is in itself sufficient for happiness (αὐτάρκης ἡ ἀρετὴ πρὸς εὐδαιμονίαν). Grateful for the beauty and healthfulness of his Sabine farm, the author pronounces the true life to consist in living up to one's character. If a man, outwardly virtuous, is deterred from wrongdoing solely by dread of punishment, he is a hypocrite, "foul within, though fair without, in his comely skin" (*introrsum turpem, speciosum pelle decora*). To harbor evil designs is to be enslaved by base passions and to lack freedom. "The good man's hatred of sin is due to love of virtue" (*oderunt peccare boni virtutis amore*). Here, in what Courbaud calls "la pièce maîtresse" of the *Epistles*, Horatian ethics rise above self-regarding morality, and reach their high-water social mark by the impulse of Stoic thought.

Throughout his *sermones*, by a prevailing spirit of geniality and tolerance toward human imperfection, Horace, without seeming too obviously to preach or denounce, succeeds in pointing out to an errant society the more excellent way.

CHAPTER V

MENIPPEAN SATIRE—
VARRO, SENECA, PETRONIUS

*Alterum illud etiam prius saturae genus sed non sola carminum varietate
mixtum condidit Terentius Varro, vir Romanorum eruditissimus.*
QUINTILIAN *Inst. Or.* X. i. 95

MENIPPEAN SATIRE, which Quintilian regarded as an older
type than Lucilian, has been touched upon in connection
with Menippus of Gadara, after whom this blend of various
meters with prose has been named. It had three exponents
in the Roman classical period: first, M. Terentius Varro, of
Reate in the Sabine country, called "Reatinus" to distinguish him from his Gallic namesake Varro "Atacinus" to
whom Horace refers as having been unsuccessful in his attempts at satire;[1] secondly, Seneca, the philosopher, in his
skit on the recently deceased Emperor Claudius; and, thirdly,
Petronius, Nero's master of ceremonies, who wrote in his
Satyricon the first picaresque novel. These three will monopo-
lize our attention in this chapter; but it is right to point out
the continuance of the Menippean form in what I have called
elsewhere the "pedantic fantasia" by Martianus Capella in
the fifth century A.D., "On the Marriage of Philology and
Mercury" (*De Nuptiis Philologiae et Mercurii*). That quaint
educational handbook had considerable literary vogue in
the Middle Ages. Another figure in the later tradition is
Boethius, who, in the sixth century, beguiled the tedium of
his melancholy imprisonment by diversifying the prose of
his *De Consolatione Philosophiae* with snatches of lyric verse.
The title and, to some extent, the form were revived at the
end of the sixteenth century in the French *Satyre Menippée*,
which, in its composite authorship, made a literary and political adjunct to the Battle of Ivry and thus signalized the
victory of Henri IV over the Catholic League.

[84]

Of the three with whom we are concerned, Varro belonged
to the Sullan and Ciceronian period, Seneca and Petronius
to the Neronian. Varro (116-27 B.C.), "most learned of the
Romans," as he has been deservedly called by Quintilian,
in his long life combined official, military, and naval duties
with enormous literary activity. A diligence unsurpassed
even by the elder Pliny in Flavian times bore fruit in what,
when seventy-eight years old, he computed at four hundred
and ninety books, "seventy hebdomads"[2] on a wide range
of subjects—history, archaeology, philosophy and philology,
physics, and agriculture. He wrote one hundred and fifty
books of *Menippean Satires*[3] besides four books of other satires, and he showed skill in various forms of verse. One of
his great repositories of knowledge, the *Antiquitates*, now
lost, was much used by St. Augustine; but time has left us
only his *Agriculture* (*Res Rusticae*) in three books, six books
from his *De Lingua Latina*, and fragments amounting to
about six hundred lines of his *Saturae Menippeae*. It is a
testimony to his impressively wide scholarship that Cicero,
not easily abashed, stood in awe of him. When the orator
wrote letters to ordinary people, he was content to have
long passages taken down in shorthand by his faithful secre-
tary Tiro, but when it came to framing an epistle to Varro,
careful phrasing was imperative and it was dictated syllable
by syllable to an underclerk.[4] Was he not the eminent poly-
math whose authority settled the canon of genuine Plautine
plays? Was it not particularly with the desire to consult
Varro's works that Cicero, when engaged on the *De Republica*,
asked permission to use Atticus' library? He recognized in
the dedication of Varro's *De Lingua Latina* to himself an
honor equal to the permission to dedicate his own *Academica* to Varro; and, in arranging for the handsome presentation copy, Cicero, overcome by a timidity about its reception,
could not avoid quoting to himself and applying to Varro a
Homeric line to this effect—"a dread man he is who might

well blame one that is blameless." Strictness of judgment, then, was added to his erudition—two qualities not uncommon in an ancient satirist.

It is a thousand pities that we have no single satire by Varro complete. We should, for instance, have been vastly curious to see how his lost *Baiae* treated that seaside resort of Clodia and the fast set in Rome. His titles—and many have had subtitles, more or less explanatory, added in Greek—are among the most original things in ancient literature, and whet a curiosity which the meager fragments cannot satisfy. "The Dish Finds Its Lid," a title in Greek ($\epsilon\hat{\upsilon}\rho\epsilon\nu$ $\dot{\eta}$ $\lambda o\pi\grave{a}s$ $\tau\grave{o}$ $\pi\hat{\omega}\mu a$), is on married people, who do sometimes "put the lid on"; "A Pot Has Its Limits" (*Est Modus Matulae*) is on drunkenness; and "I've Got You" ($\check{\epsilon}\chi\omega$ $\sigma\epsilon$) is, rather cryptically, on Fortune. "A Ulysses and a Half" (*Sesculixes*) may treat of the wanderer over the fields of thought who must, in that infinite realm, exceed the ten years of the epic hero's geographical *Odyssey*. And many others are equally intriguing: "But Does There Not Await You—?" ($\dot{a}\lambda\lambda$' $o\dot{\upsilon}$ $\mu\acute{\epsilon}\nu\epsilon\iota$ $\sigma\epsilon$;) what? presumably, to use Gray's words, the inevitable hour; "Man-Town" ($'A\nu\theta\rho\omega\pi\acute{o}\pi o\lambda\iota s$) pictures family life; "Aborigines" is on the development of human nature: a line in it, "the old donkey isn't better than the young one," enforces the truth that virtue is not the certain companion of gray hairs. Several titles introduce the author's praenomen, like *Marcopolis*, "Marcus'Town"; *Marcipor*, "Marcus' Slave" or possibly "Marcus' Child"; and *Bimarcus*, "The Twain Marks" or "Mark in Twain," where Varro, thinking Pirandello-like of twofold personality, makes the old-fashioned Marcus of the Roman past hold converse with his new self, the other Marcus, belonging to the Roman present. "The Battle of the Goats" (*Caprinum Proelium*) is on pleasure; "The Swan" (*Cycnus*), perhaps, in Tennyson's words, "fluting a wild carol ere her death," is on burial; "Until When?" ($\check{\epsilon}\omega s$ $\pi o\tau\epsilon$;), on the flight of time; "The Teacher of the Old" (γεροντοδιδάσκαλος), a study of past and present; "The World-Borer" (κοσμοτορύνη), a drill—much worse than the noisiest street-drill—gradually destroying the universe;"An Ajax of Straw" (*Aiax Stramenticius*), which may or may not be a burlesque of tragedy. "Old Up-in-the-Morning" (*Manius*) is the householder who knows how to work his slaves;"The Dry Measure"(*Modius*) plays with thoughts on the observance of due measure (*modus*) in life; "Mules Scratch Mules' Backs" (*Mutuum Muli Scabunt*),which suggests log rolling, has the unexpected subtitle περὶ χωρισμοῦ, apparently on the severance of body from soul. "When an Ass Hears the Lyre" (ὄνος λύρας) touches on music, an art usually disdained by Cynics; "Oh My! Oh My!" or "Well, I Never!" (*Papiapapae*) professes to express wonderment at silly flatteries, and the opposite fault of unfair censure, and "The False Apollo" (*Pseudulus Apollo*) attacks the Egyptian god Serapis.

Even this bare selection from the surviving titles indicates his range. Several satires can be reconstructed, although there is the handicap inherent in the uncertain order of the fragments, in the sudden transitions of thought favored by *satura*, and in the incalculable factor of the author's quaint fantasy. One of the *saturae* of which we can get a full and connected idea is that with the engaging title,"Thou Knowest Not What the Late Eventide Brings"(*Nescis quid vesper serus vehat*). Here Gellius comes to the rescue. From Gellius (XIII. xi), who quotes parts of it, we learn that it contained a sort of code for dinner parties. Guests should range in number from that of the Graces, three, to that of the Muses, nine— any more make a troublesome crowd. The four essentials for a successful dinner are the right sort of guests, the right place, the right time, and the right menu. Guests should not be chatterboxes, yet not dumb either; for eloquence is proper in the forum or in a law court, whereas silence befits rather one's bedroom than a festive party. What Varro lays down

here about *sermones* is of obvious interest in a study of satire.
Subjects of conversation at dinner, he feels, should not be
worrying or perplexing; they should be pleasant and attractive (*invitabiles*), combining profit with charm, so as to im-
prove the mind. This will result, if we confine our talk to
ordinary concerns of life which we have no time to discuss
in business hours. The host need not cut a fashionable figure,
but must be free from vulgarity. What is read at a dinner
party should be at once pleasurable and give help in life
(βιωφελῆ). Nor does Varro fail to prescribe concerning des-
sert (*de secundis mensis*), and Gellius quotes his words to the
effect that, "Those sweets are sweetest which are not sweet-
ened to excess; for there is but an untrustworthy alliance
between delicacies and a delicate digestion!" (πέμμασιν enim
cum πέψει societas infida). Another satire touched on by
Gellius, VII. xvi, is on the kindred theme of dainty dishes
(περὶ ἐδεσμάτων) of fish and flesh available for the table from
far-sundered cities in the Roman dominions—peacock from
Samos, woodcock from Phrygia, kids from Ambracia, tunny
from Chalcedon, oysters from Tarentum, nuts from Thasos,
dates from Egypt, and so on. Summing these up as *cibi pere-
grini et lautitiae*, Varro stigmatizes the hunt for luxurious
foods all over the world. To this satire belongs his reproof:
"If you'd given a twelfth of the attention to philosophy which
you've devoted to getting your baker to bake good bread,
you'd have been a good man yourself long ago."[5]

Yet another satire whose outline can be reconstructed is
entitled *Sexagessis*, "Sixty Years Old." This is Varro's Rip
van Winkle, who fell asleep at the age of ten and awoke half
a century afterward to find Rome absolutely changed. He
has himself undergone a metamorphosis: instead of the shorn
head of his boyhood he has now a bald pate and bristles like
a hedgehog's and a huge snout (*cum proboscide*). The place
of time-honored virtues has been taken by the arrival of new
denizens (*inquilinae*)—Impiety, Perfidy, Shamelessness. His

free comments on the signs of deterioration give such offense that it is proposed to throw the old man from one of the bridges into the Tiber.

Gellius tells an amusing story of a conceited fellow in a bookseller's shop who boasted that he alone under wide heaven could explain why the satires of Varro were called "Cynic" by some and "Menippean" by the author.[6] There happened to be available a book of his satires entitled Ὑδροκύων, "The Water-Dog"; so, by way of test, Gellius confronted the braggart with a passage which he, after some demur, was induced to read. He did it badly enough to make the bystanders giggle; then stopped and pleaded bad eyesight. "But at any rate," urged Gellius, "do tell me what does *caninum prandium* in that passage mean?" The blockhead got up and, as he went, said, "A big question! *I* don't explain such points without a fee" (*talia ego gratis non doceo*). Gellius and his friends, after some discussion, settled that *caninum prandium* meant "a dog's lunch," one in fact without any wine. The title of the *satura* itself, Ὑδροκύων, and other titles like Ἱπποκύων, "Horse-Dog"; κυνοδιδάσκαλος, "Dog-Teacher"; κυνορήτωρ, "Dog-Speaker," and the Latinized *Cynicus*, go some way toward explaining the term "Cynicae" applied in Gellius to Varro's *Saturae*. A similar interest in Cynicism, the snarling, dog-in-the-manger philosophy, accounts for Varro's writing "The Burial of Menippus" (ταφὴ Μενίππου),[7] where those present praise the dead Cynic (*ille nobilis quondam canis*) and turn to a eulogy upon the good old times.

Altogether his hundred and fifty books of Menippean satires, distinct from four other books of satires, made a wonderful miscellany, reflecting the life of the age, its social foibles, its philosophical disputes, its literary interests, sometimes its Oriental religions and political upheavals, all conveyed in the varying forms of monologue and dialogue, of narrative and fable, of realistic descriptions or imaginary flights into Utopias. The sympathies of the old-fashioned

Roman gentleman with the simpler past and his distrust of dogmatic systems of philosophy are unmistakable. His *Eumenides* forcibly expressed the Cynic pronouncement on the quarreling schools of thought: "No sick man's monstrous dream can be so wild that some philosopher won't say it's true."[9] At the same time, it was his desire to convey pleasantly to the ordinary man a practical scheme of conduct.[10]

Mainly his satires were among his earlier works: Cichorius thinks they were written between 81 and 67 B.C. But though Varro grew more serious as time went by, and the graver element gradually ousted the facetious, some satires are clearly later. "The Three-headed Monster," Τρικάρανος,[11] showed his hostility to the Coalition of Caesar, Pompey, and Crassus in 60 B.C.; *Sexagessis* seems a personal allusion to his sixtieth year; and there is reason to think that his *Tithonus* is later than Cicero's *De Senectute*.[12]

While his model in a broad sense was Menippus, Varro was also influenced by Ennius in the form of his *satura*, by Accius in his study of literary questions, by Plautus in his language, and by Lucilius in some of his tone as well as in language. He quotes from Lucilius several times without naming him,[13] and he names both Ennius and Plautus in borrowing expressions from them.[14] But, after all, he was the maker of his own vigorous language, knotty and gnarled it may be, but picturesque in the effect secured sometimes by old words, sometimes by words like *caballus* from the common speech, sometimes by literary artifices like alliteration. His variety of verse-forms[15] shows a suppleness in composition, influenced by older Latin writers and by the neoteric school of poetry. His iambics are well represented in his powerful description of a rainstorm in the *Marcipor*, pieced together out of different citations found in Nonius.[16] His animation of style is seen in both prose and verse. To illustrate the former I translate his scathing sentence about cheap sympathy with a man defeated in a boxing match: "The pugilist may say: 'You spectators, who think it a wretched thing to be beaten, I ask you, if my opponent scrapes my eyebrows off with his boxing gloves, is there any one among you ready to give me his?' "[17] To illustrate his iambics I translate a quatrain in praise of wine into octosyllabics:

> None quaffs a merrier drink than wine:
> 'Tis made to cure the hearts that pine—
> The seed-plot sweet of jollity,
> The bond that binds the banquet-glee.

> (*Vino nihil iucundius quisquam bibit.*
> *hoc aegritudinem ad medendam invenerunt,*
> *hoc hilaritatis dulce seminarium,*
> *hoc continet coagulum convivia.*)[18]

This belongs to the satire upon drunkenness. It would have been most entertaining to know how Varro worked out his scheme so as not to leave the topers with the last word.

To find the staid philosopher L. Annaeus Seneca (*ca.* 4 B.C.–65 A.D.) also among the satirists has so startled some scholars that they have solved their difficulty by denying[19] his authorship of the *Apocolocyntosis* or "Pumpkinification" of the Emperor Claudius, in which Claudius is ejected from heaven and sent back by way of earth to Hades. This is, however, to ignore manuscript testimony and, as far as style goes, to overlook the capacity for humor which he shows from time to time in his letters to his friend Lucilius Junior, besides his skill in verse writing as seen in his tragedies and in most, if not all, of seventy-three brief poems plausibly ascribed to him from the *Anthologia Latina.* Seneca was a versatile writer, and much in the Emperor Claudius' conduct rankled in his heart enough to impel him to a post-mortem attack. One part of the objection turns on the title. Dio Cassius[20] records Seneca's writing a "Pumpkinification" (ἀποκολοκύντωσις) with a verbal play on "Deification" (ἀπαθανάτισις), but the title in the best manuscript, the Sangallensis, *Divi Claudii incipit Apotheosis* (spelt Ἀποθήοσις) *Annei Senece per sati-ram*, does not agree with this until we realize, with Buecheler, that it is a telltale fusion of an original title *Divi Claudii Apocolocyntosis* with its gloss *Apotheosis per satiram* which was designed to explain the parody in the strange word *Apo-colocyntosis*, meaning "Pumpkinification." Further difficulty is felt because Claudius is not actually turned into a pump-kin. True, but Claudius in the Roman view was a pumpkin or silly ass all the time, and instead of getting deified he was shown up as a blockhead. The satiric use of the Latin *cucur-bita*, corresponding to the Greek κολοκύντη, is well authen-ticated.[21]

If the skit did not follow closely upon Claudius' death in October 54 A.D., its composition may be connected with Nero's annulment of Claudius' consecration.[22] There is no room here to give full details of this clever and amusing account of how Claudius "bubbled out the ghost" and how he fared with his application in heaven to be enrolled as a god. But some aspects must be touched on. The *Apocolocyntosis*,[23] while it is a satire on deification, is also a parody on the writing of history, and the point of the sting is that Claudius plumed himself on being a historian. It pretends in Lucianesque style to be a *vera historia*. The author professes to tell the truth; yet, in the next breath, he declares he will say what comes first into his mouth (*dicam quod mihi in buccam venerit*), and asks ironically who ever required from the historian wit-nesses to support him. His authority for the true tale is one who, will he nill he, must see everything that is done in heaven, in which asseveration Seneca goes one better than the ordinary satirist, whose customary scene is earth and whose theme the wickedness thereof. But the true tale is to be told as a secret: "Question him, he'll give you the story, when you're alone: before a lot of people, he'll never give you a word!" This mock-serious introduction is good fooling and aptly drives home the spirit of burlesque. The fun be-

gins on earth.Why did the Emperor take an unconscionable
time in dying? Well, one of the Fates wanted to give him a
little more time to extend Roman citizenship to the few aliens
whom Claudius' indiscriminate franchise policy had left
without it! When, however, Mercury remonstrates with the
Fates that it is too bad to let the old man go on gasping as
he had done for sixty-four years, Clotho agrees to end his
mortal troubles:

> Round the foul spindle then she twined the thread
> And snipped the life span of Prince Dunderhead.[24]

Lachesis meanwhile has a golden thread for the new emperor,
and Apollo is charmed with Nero's similarity to himself in
looks and voice and song.When the scene changes to heaven,
Claudius' shambling gait, stammering utterance, and shak-
ing head make him a complete puzzle on his arrival. No one
can understand the imperial pedant's language; no one dreams
that it could be Latin; so Hercules, as a great traveler, is
sent by Jupiter to question him. Seeing that the stranger had
something like the look of a human being (*visus est quasi
homo*), Hercules fired Greek at him, a Homeric line which
Claudius capped with glee over the learning in heaven. It
promised some vogue for his own works in history among
celestial readers—another hit at Claudius' scholarship.

From this point the vital question in the *Apocolocyntosis*
is, Shall Claudius be deified, or shall he not? Though a personal lampoon in its contemptuous ridicule of the recently
deceased emperor, it was an implicit satire on the whole idea
of apotheosis. Its Stoic author could not but recollect with
disfavor the attempts of Caligula to usurp the honors due to
Jupiter from officiating priests.[25] There was need for the sol-
vent of satire. Not many years had to pass before Galba
sought to trace his lineage back to Pasiphaë, daughter of the
Sun-God, clearly as a step toward deification. So here Seneca
pours ridicule on such notions by a treatment of the debat-

ing Olympians as flippant as any atheistic Epicurean could
desire.When Claudius is imagined to have enlisted the good
offices of Hercules to tout for his enrollment in the celestial
company, the author aims at undermining the system of
deifying emperors. Claudius' prospects are utterly ruined by
Augustus, who rises to oppose the motion that this queer
and scarcely intelligible newcomer should be admitted into
the divine circle. Now Augustus, as best of the emperors so
far, deserved deification, if any Roman ruler did, but his
words by no means exalt the dignity of the gods. He has been
most considerate, he remarks: he has never troubled his
brother gods till now that he is making his maiden speech in
their illustrious House. The irony of the skit reaches its cul-
mination in the rejection of Claudius by the great predecessor whose name had been frequently on his lips. Augustus
can no longer conceal his anger, he says.This miserable creature has undone Augustus' policy of peace on land and sea
and of coöperation with the Senate: he has revelled in death
sentences, often in cases which were untried. That is not
proper usage, at least not in heaven; "For consider Jupiter.
For all the years he has been ruler, Vulcan is the only person
whose leg he ever broke! He may have strung his wife up,
but you can't say he killed her!"Finally, Augustus makes
the point that nobody is likely to worship such a thing as
Claudius. Make *him* a god and nobody would believe in the
gods themselves!

These arguments prove decisive. Deportation instead of
apotheosis is the verdict. The scene changes to earth, where
Claudius recognizes his own funeral—a most lovely funeral
(*formosissimum*), and so elaborate in ceremonial that, as
Seneca says with effective irony on the very point in dispute,
you could plainly grasp that these were the obsequies of a
god (*plane ut scires deum efferri*).The music of the anapaestic
dirge fascinates the spectator, but his conductor Mercury
orders him to continue their journey. So once more the scene

changes. In Hades it is easy going down: a twinkle, and Claudius, though gouty, was at Pluto's door. As Narcissus, his freedman, had announced his coming, Claudius is met by a crowd of his victims, consuls, prefects, relatives, freedmen. How, asked the absent-minded prince, were all his friends there? An angry howl replies that he as their murderer had sent them thither. They demand justice from Aeacus. He is haled then into court, where Aeacus metes out his reward on the Claudian system of hearing one side only, the prosecution. Sentence: to rattle dice in a bottomless dice-box to all eternity. Just then Caligula appears and claims his imperial uncle as a runaway slave. Witnesses testify to having seen him beaten by Caligula; and that is taken to prove his servitude. Adjudged therefore to Caligula, he is by him given back to the righteous judge Aeacus and by Aeacus handed over to his Greek freedman Menander to act as a law clerk in court forevermore.

The conclusion has been criticized. It has been thought abrupt enough to indicate that the satire is unfinished, and it has been thought an inappropriate punishment. These comments fail to take into account both the traditions of satire and the personal history of the Emperor. Satires often ended abruptly, as may be seen in the first, ninth, and tenth of Horace's first book; and as for Claudius' penalty, could anything be more suitable than that this emperor who had on earth almost a mania for sitting on the bench at trials should now have more than his fill of court procedure by being condemned to be an underclerk at trials for all eternity in hell? Further, is he not fittingly made subject to a freedman, as freedmen ruled at court during his reign?

This lampoon was a very different production from Seneca's flatteries of the Emperor when he sent from exile in 43 A.D. to the important court-freedman Polybius a *Consolation* on a brother's death. Momigliano[26] has indeed remarked affinities between the two works, as he considers that the

Consolation has a harsh note in its ironical contrast between
the exalted position of Polybius and the mere idea of his
needing comfort; but the general contrast is more obvious.
Seneca's Stoicism was not untouched by inconsistency.
Though he had written an obituary panegyric on Claudius
for Nero to deliver, it clearly gave him a human satisfaction
to send the Emperor to hell as he now did in his pasquinade:
nor is it at all unlikely that the hint to write the skit came
from the young prince himself. For Nero too had a satiric
bent. We know from Tacitus that he composed a verse attack upon the immorality of Afranius Quintianus, and from
Suetonius we know of another by him, entitled "The One-
Eyed Man," which was directed against the former praetor
Clodius Pollio, a man of bad character.[27] Besides, it was
among the aims of the satire, through its compliments to
Nero, to herald a better age in Rome under the auspices of
the imperial pupil in whom Seneca reposed high hopes and
on whom he desired to exercise a beneficial influence.

Resuscitating the Menippean manner in its flight to heaven
and its cavalier treatment of gods and heroes, Seneca's satire also owes something to Lucilius and to Varro. But it is
thoroughly original. There is no other such lampoon in Latin. Its interest is not social, as is the interest of Varro and
Petronius, and, to a high degree, of Seneca himself in his
Epistulae. It produced two imitations long afterward: Lipsius' *Satura Menippea*, toward the end of the sixteenth century; and, in 1612, the *Sardi Venales* of Cunaeus.

A very different type of satire from Seneca's is the picture
of low society given in the *Satyricon*[28] (originally a Greek
genitive plural) by Petronius.[29] He is by general consent
identified with Nero's aristocratic adviser on social etiquette,
his *arbiter elegantiarum*, to whose career and suicide (66 A.D.)
Tacitus assigns two chapters in his *Annals*.[30] "Energy makes
some men's reputation," says the historian, "but idling had
made his"; yet, devotee of polished luxury as he was, Pe-

tronius had shown himself alert and businesslike when governor of Bithynia. That he was keenly penetrating in observation his great realistic romance affords constant proof.

The surviving portions (and they are not free from gaps) belong only to Books XV and XVI of a long narrative relating the travels and adventures of three unprincipled scapegraces, Encolpius, Ascyltus, and Giton, not in Rome, but, what lends it special attraction, in different Greek cities of Campania and Southern Italy. Apparently the scene of some of the lost portions was laid in Massilia.[31] What we still have begins apparently at Cumae; and Encolpius, a young freedman of better education than character, is represented as giving his personal account, in the first person, of events which befell himself and his two disreputable comrades. They bear Greek names[32] whose sense might in a modern book be expressed as M. Embrasseur, M. Sain-et-sauf, and M. Voisin. The work consists, not of brief separate sketches as in Varro, but of a continuous story whose various episodes are linked together by the reappearance of certain characters. This perhaps gives it all the unity needed without calling in a burlesque "Wrath of Priapus" to give a slender thread of connection throughout. Its framework is the irresponsible vagabondage of the two beggar-students with a scampish hanger-on, the boy, Giton—conscienceless rascals journeying from inn to inn, drinking, brawling, stealing, rivals in nameless vice, stained with crime, half bullies and half poltroons. It is thus the first picaresque novel, an ancient *Gil Blas* or *Roderick Random*. The sexuality of the *Satyricon* is unbridled and unashamed. The two students are in their knaveries and lewdness nakedly devoid of scruple. We might as well apply a moral scale-measure to a thunderstorm or a typhoon as to their delinquencies. All the same, Encolpius has ability enough to declaim against contemporary education and is answered by Professor Agamemnon, who places its defects at the doors of parents in their demand for quick results. Agamemnon

ends his harangue with verses in the Lucilian manner, and
he it is who, after the ragged students have passed through
a series of the shadiest adventures, brings them to Trimalchio's dinner party, which is the most important surviving
part of Petronius.

The menu was one long succession of the most lavish
courses, in which the element of surprise played a great part,
as in the wooden hen sitting on egg-shaped dainties; or the
round dish divided and garnished according to the signs of
the Zodiac; or the huntsmen with hounds and with a tray
bearing a wild sow which is slit open to let thrushes out; or a
pig brought in apparently ungutted, but, when carved, found
to be full of sausages and black puddings. This sort of extravagant bounty leaves the guests with jaded appetites
long before Trimalchio's kitchen is exhausted. There is wine
to match, excellent old Falernian, labeled "100 years in
bottle." The atmosphere of display is everywhere around
—wine, not water, to wash the hands in; a slave boy boxed
for troubling to pick up a silver entrée dish he had let drop;
the host's personal adornment; inscriptions with his name
on pillars and on the silver; pictures of his career from slave
market to affluence. The figure of Trimalchio is cast in almost
an epic mold. He is the center of the realism in the story of
the banquet, a convincing picture of vulgar success. Petronius succeeds in making his Trimalchio a figure of fun as unforgettable as are Cervantes' Don Quixote and Shakespeare's
Falstaff. Of the three Trimalchio is the most natural; for
there is more suggestion of caricature in the portrayal of
the other two. He never loses his hold on our attention from
the moment when, before the party, we get our first glimpse
of him—"a bald old man in a reddish shirt, playing at a game
in which he never stooped to pick a ball up if it touched the
ground, but had a slave to supply fresh ones from a bag."
We expect ill-bred remarks from him. He tells his guests that
he had found it inconvenient to come so soon to dinner, and

that he had entertained more important people the day before, but gave them poorer wine. He puts questions to his cook before the guests which are intended to impress them with the number of his slaves; and they have to listen to the reminiscences, reflections, and finances of a self-made man, and, toward the close, when he is in a maudlin state, to his arrangements for his funeral and the inscription on his tomb. Though he had drafted in his epitaph a sentence that he had never gone to lectures, he would not be thought to despise learning entirely; for he intimated that he possessed two libraries, a Greek and a Latin. What, however, he tried to learn had left his mind in a muddle: Hannibal according to him was at Troy, and he confuses Cassandra with Medea. Yet Trimalchio is not without wit. When Agamemnon tells him that his declamation for the day had for its text or title, "A poor man and a rich man were once at enmity," he asks with delightful innocence, "What is a poor man?"[33]

Drawn with less detail, the other characters in the dining room are yet thoroughly natural figures. The host's wife, Fortunata, a keen managing person with pronounced likes and dislikes, is the able controller, because the brains, of the household. When Habinnas, a maker of tombstones and a rough brute, appears on the scene bringing his wife, Scintilla (Madame Spark), from a funeral feast at which there have been liberal potations, the hostess is sent for to welcome her, and the two women are soon engaged in exchanging boasts about their finery.

But nothing brings one nearer to the party than to listen to the conversation of the *colliberti* invited to it. Their conversation mixes mere twaddle with inane platitudes and bad grammar. Listen to Dama, who has been calling for bumpers of wine:

"Day," he solemnly declares, "is nothing: before you can turn, it's night. So there isn't anything better than to go straight from bed to the dining room. And we've had a tidy frost." (His utterance thickens and his grammar weakens.) "A bath shcareshly warmed me up. After all, a hot drink puts a wrapper round you. I've swigged neat wine and am absholutely tipshy (*plane matus*). Wine'sh gone to my head (*vinus mihi in cerebrum abit*)";[34] and he mixes his genders as he most likely had mixed his drinks.

Another guest follows up the cue about a bath: "*I* don't go in for a bath every day: the bath attendant works you as a fuller does clothes, and the water has a bite (*aqua dentes habet*). . . . Besides, I couldn't have any bath: I was at a funeral today."[35] Then follow his remarks on the deceased: "Killed by doctors; well, no," he corrects himself, "just by unkind fate. (His gender is wrong, *malus fatus*.) However, he had a fine procession, and the mourning was tip-top—he had left a lot of slaves their freedom—even if the widow was stingy with her weeping."

His chatter is taken up by Phileros, who has further details to give; and he is bound to speak the truth because he has eaten the dog's tongue (*linguam caninam*): the deceased "had a rough mouth, gabbled for ever, and was quarrelsomeness incarnate" (*discordia, non homo*). He had a brother with whom he disagreed, and left property out of the family, on which Varro's title is quoted, "Whoever flees from his own folk has a long way to flee" (*longe fugit quisquis suos fugit*).[36]

Then yet another guest, Ganymede, utters a growl on dear food. He can recall gentlemen of the good old sort who helped to keep things right, Safinius, for example, hot stuff, "more pepper than man (*piper non homo*), he scorched the ground wherever he went," but a straight, dependable man, whose voice rose in court like a trumpet, and who showed courtesy in returning a greeting and in calling everybody by name "just like one of ourselves. These were times when food was dirt cheap. . . . Now things grow worse every day. This town of ours grows downward as does a calf's tail."[37] By way of contrast, Echion is an optimist and rattles on about gladiatorial shows. Conscious of the infirmity of his own Latin, he twits Professor Agamemnon with his silence: "Folks like you that's able to speak, doesn't (*tu qui potes loquere non loquis*). You're not in our set, and that's why you make fun of we poor people."[38] In much of this easygoing talk can be heard unmistakable echoes of everyday speech with an admixture of Greek words inevitable in the language of freedmen in South Italy.[39]

Recitations and other performances diversify the entertainment. Niceros tells, by request, his eerie story of a werewolf, and this is succeeded by the host's creepy tale about witches putting a straw changeling in the place of a boy.[40] The third story thus inserted within the story is that of "The Widow of Ephesus," told by Eumolpus, when the narrative is continued after the banquet, to illustrate the fickleness of women.[41] But the viands, the liquor, the amusements provided could not fail to weary the guests. The trio of associates had been planning to leave, but not until a slave's trumpet brought an unexpected visit from the Fire Brigade could they escape in the early morning. Their adventures are resumed. Encolpius, who has quarreled with Ascyltus over Giton, meets the reprobate old poet Eumolpus; and with him the three, having patched up their quarrel, embark on a voyage, when to their alarm they discover aboard the same ship two enemies, Lichas, who had appeared in the earlier missing part of the novel, and the courtesan Tryphaena. We must pass over their unsuccessful attempts at disguise, the storm at sea which rid them of their enemy Lichas, the arrival of the quartette at Crotona, where the chief industry was legacy hunting, and their adaptation to environment by their entrance on an elaborate scheme of willful fraud and imposture.

Just as Nero's depraved fancy craved for amusement in the slums of Rome, so a jaded sensualist like Petronius discovered a piquancy in his imaginative picture of rascality

and vulgarity among characters and scenes which were in
contrast with those in court circles, where Petronius himself
cut a figure as ultimate authority on what was socially correct. To break away from cultivated Latin, to reproduce by
a *tour de force* the slang, the bad grammar, the inanities but
at the same time the pithiness of plebeian Latin as spoken
by Trimalchio's guests was a refreshing relief for a clever literary man who could, when he preferred, write good Latin
prose, and versify in several different manners.[42] But it was
not only their language which made entertaining "copy."
Their bourgeois ways amused the observant nobleman; and
his satire consists in the ingenious choice of realistic detail,
just enough and not too much to be artistic. Petronius allows
his characters to speak and act for themselves. His ridicule
depends not on comment, but on discerning presentation—
that most powerful realism which, as we are reminded in the
preface to Guy de Maupassant's *Pierre et Jean*, is not photog-
raphy but the selection made by genius. Preserving an im-
partial aloofness from his squalid personages, he neither
condemns nor commends. But it is impossible to believe he
could have said, as some modern novelists say with doubtful
logicality, "The characters in this book are entirely imaginary, and have no relation to any living person." He must
have drawn upon his own observation and experience: and
yet the personal note is withheld. The narrative is told with
invariable restraint; and this makes him one of the best of
storytellers, whether he is using his own observation or re-
furbishing a Milesian tale like that of the Ephesian widow.

Petronius' novel is in the lineage of Menippean satire.
With less philosophy and more gaiety, the satirical romance
could appeal to a wider public of readers.[43] There have been
various endeavors to discover sources of influence on Petronius in the heroic romance, in some of the stories which
come into the elder Seneca's collection of rhetorical debates,
in the prologue of comedies, in the realism of the mime, and

in erotic Milesian tales, whether in Greek or in Sisenna's Latin adaptations from Aristides. Some of these, like the Milesian tales,[44] obviously affected Petronius; but it is hard to see much in the theory which would explain the *Satyricon* as mainly a travesty of Greek love-romances. Whatever its borrowings,—and in an author of wide culture like Petronius they were many,—the novel stands on its own merits as a creation of independent genius. It does not lessen his originality that Petronius can quote Virgil and Horace, and Trimalchio's dinner party, though influenced by that of Nasidienus in Horace, remains Petronius' own work.[45] Indeed, it is significant to note how fresh is his treatment of this *Cena*-motif handed over as a stock feature from Greek to Latin, and how brilliantly he handles the already established features of a vulgar parvenu, overlavish display, an accident during the feast, the guests' difficulty to avoid laughing at their entertainer, and their free conversation during his temporary withdrawal. Similarly with another commonplace of satire, the *captatores* or legacy hunters, whom we meet in Horace, Persius, and afterward in Juvenal: this old theme, bequeathed from the time of Menippus, is given fresh treatment in the imaginary conception of a city whose population was divided between *captatores* and *captati*.[46]

Yet another theme usual in Roman satire turns on literary questions. Trimalchio's amusing blunders are a parody on literary knowledge, but points of far-reaching importance are raised in Encolpius' declamation on the decay of eloquence with Agamemnon's reply to his tirade,[47] and again in Eumolpus' reflections upon poetry.[48] These last introduce the two hundred and ninety-five hexameters[49] on the Civil War of 49 B.C., the outcome of the rivalry among three *duces* whose doom is summarized in lines 63-64 of the poem:

> The grave of Crassus is in Parthia;
> Great Pompey lieth on the Libyan shore,
> And Julius drenched ungrateful Rome with gore.[50]

The poem, proving Petronius' versatility, though given with
the apology that it had not received the final touch, conveys
an implicit criticism on Lucan's historical epic for such
features as its abandonment of divine interventions, and
has a few clever echoes of his epigrammatic style. It is
through Eumolpus that Petronius sums up Horace's quest of
the *mot juste* as "a studied happiness of phrase," the *curiosa
felicitas* which everyone remembers.

The other great fictitious narrative in Latin prose, the
Metamorphoses, or *Golden Ass*, of Apuleius, lies outside our
chronological limits and contains too little verse to be strictly
Menippean. Later yet, *The Marriage of Philology and Mercury*, while still Menippean in form, is allegorical and therefore in a different category. Both the *Satyricon* and the
Golden Ass are more vividly entertaining than the stereotyped adventures of lovers in the romances which were to
have a vogue in Greek; but the *Satyricon* is the more original
and the more Roman work. The *Golden Ass* owes a deeper
debt to Milesian tales, especially in the charming fairy story
of Cupid and Psyche. No doubt there is satiric intention in
Apuleius' introduction into the general narrative of prevalent superstition, sacerdotal chicanery, and triumphant brig-
andage; but its marvels and magic produce an atmosphere
dissimilar to the realism which permeates the *Satyricon*. Even
where the realism of Apuleius is marked, his bizarre African
Latinity contrasts with the straightforward style of Petronius, whose ear was alert to catch, if need be, the very accents
of low life.

The three works considered in this chapter, Varro's *Menippeae*, Seneca's *Apocolocyntosis*, and Petronius' *Satyricon*, are
naturally linked together by resemblance in their blend of
prose and verse, in their borrowings from the common speech
and proverbial lore, in their introduction of parodies on the
grand style, and in their use of irony at the expense of gods
and mythology. But they present differences. Varro, though

disdainful of wild theorizing, harbored an honest desire to pass on to readers some of his own philosophic learning. Seneca was for the time being unphilosophic enough to let his hot resentment against Claudius find vent in vindictive acerbity. Petronius, with a disregard for decency which was perhaps partly prompted by the traditional Cynic outspokenness, showed himself so much a master of realism that his characters produce the illusive impression of life and action independent of their author.

CHAPTER VI

PHAEDRUS AND PERSIUS—
BEAST FABLE AND STOIC HOMILY

Duplex libelli dos est: quod risum movet
et quod prudenti vitam consilio monet
PHAEDRUS I. prol. 3-4

Ipse semipaganus
ad sacra vatum carmen adfero nostrum
PERSIUS prol. 6-7

FABLE was a traditional element in *satura*. It had been employed in the Greek diatribe to enforce a moral lesson, and in Latin by Ennius, Lucilius, and Horace. It is therefore right to examine the use made of it by the first fabulist who wrote separate collections of fables in Latin—Phaedrus.[1]

Whether the original stimulus to invent fables, and especially the beast story which had a vogue amid the folklore of the East, lay in some dim latent totemism or simply in the impulse toward imaginative creation and the desire to entertain, or whether there was from the outset the purpose of sage instruction, is indeterminable. It is difficult to tell an imaginary tale about bees or ants without implicitly suggesting analogies with diligent and provident human beings and differences from the slack and the improvident. When Horace[2] characterizes the tiny ant as a mighty toiler (*magni formica laboris*), adding a few lines about her habits, it is true he relates no fable, but he derives from the creature who uses her store a lesson (*nam exemplo est*) for the miser whom nothing can stop from adding endlessly to his accumulated gains, and whom he addresses with a direct reproach, "while, as for you, neither burning heat can push you aside from profitmaking, nor winter, fire, sea, nor sword" (*cum te neque fervidus aestus demoveat lucro, neque hiemps, ignis, mare, ferrum*). Just so the Scriptures[3] use the same example for a direct appeal to an idler, "Go to the ant, thou sluggard; consider her ways and be wise, which having no guide, overseer or ruler, provideth her meat in the summer and gathereth her food in the harvest. How long wilt thou sleep, O sluggard?" One might well believe here that a Stoico-Cynic was preaching.

It is, however, when personality is given to animals, when they are credited with speech and behavior, that the purpose of fable, partly didactic, partly satiric, becomes obvious. Ennius' fable of the crested lark and her nestlings hardly needs its moral pointed, that for what you want done it is better to rely on yourself than on neighbors; and Horace's elaborate "Town Mouse and Country Mouse" very plainly conveys the advantages of simple fare. So with the traditional fables which are familiar in our nurseries as household words, and which children love perhaps without being, as Reinach would have it, unconscious totemists. "The Wolf and the Lamb" rouses sympathy for innocent weakness injured by the unfair slander and brute force of the big bad wolf. Bad men are like bad beasts or worse. This is why fable stings. The satiric shaft goes home, because the plain resemblance pricks a guilty conscience.

So much merely for the moral aspect. In developed communities the beast fable can be extended to cover not only social but also political aims under a more protective disguise than is afforded by ordinary satire, even when professedly impersonal. This is one of the aims which we shall find intended, and in some quarters resented, among the fables of Phaedrus.

A Thracian alien by birth, brought early in life to Rome, he passed through the usual literary education in Greek and Latin, and his works show acquaintance with Simonides and Euripides, Ennius and Virgil. The line which he quotes from the *Telephus* of Ennius to the effect that his satire must be circumspect ("an open growl from common folk is crime") is a specific reminiscence of his school days.[4] His echoes of Euripides are particularly illuminating because they occur in a piece where, replying to the hypercriticism of detractors, he shows he can adopt the tragic style if he chooses.[5] Arguments have also been adduced for a direct knowledge of Horace on Phaedrus' part.[6] What, however, most nearly concerns us in him is the power, for which he claims originality, to turn the Aesopian fable into Latin iambics:

> If Latium look but kindly on my toil,
> More writers she shall have to match with Greece.[7]

To Phaedrus' unquestioning faith the learned Samian slave, Aesop, in the sixth century B.C. was the revered author of the whole collection of prose fables which had been gathered by Demetrius of Phaleron about 300 B.C. and which, though passing under the name of "Aesop," included many accretions assigned to him as a traditional father of the beast story. Phaedrus is frank about his debt:

> Matter which first old Aesop did rehearse
> Hath Phaedrus polished in iambic verse.
> Two boons my book hath: it can laughter raise
> And gives sage counsel in life's wildering maze.
> Howbeit, should one think to criticize,
> Since beasts, nay even trees, here sermonize,
> Let him remember that in fables we
> Divert ourselves with unreality.[8]

Two preliminary points are noticeable in this passage: first, the claim, typically common in satire, that he combines laughter (*risum movet*) with sound advice; secondly, a point which is one of several proving that we no longer have a complete Phaedrus, his allusion to trees speaking. The favorite trees of certain deities are mentioned in III. xvii, but they do not speak there or anywhere else in the extant fables.

A *libertus* in the household of Augustus, Phaedrus seems to have published his first two books in Tiberius' reign. His third book, dedicated to Eutychus, probably the charioteer of the Greens under Caligula, appeared not later than the beginning of A.D. 41. In that book, conscious of advancing years,[9] he announces his intention to stop writing; but in the prologue to the fourth book, dedicated to a literary friend Particulo, he explains his change of mind. So his last book, the fifth, is addressed to one Philetes or Philetus, and contains an allusion to an old hunting hound no longer equal to his former self any more than the author could now pretend to be.[10] The books vary in length and have suffered losses which perhaps began with the suppression of some fables by the author himself,[11] whose prologues indicate his consciousness of offense given by his writing. It is therefore doubtful whether we now possess the most stinging examples of his satire; and the prudery of medieval copyists excised certain coarsenesses which might have explained the single allusion cited as applied to him before Avianus about the end of the fourth century,[12] namely, Martial's question, "Does he vie with the jests of naughty Phaedrus?" (*an aemulatur improbi iocos Phaedri?*).[13]

The diffusion of popular preaching in the first century of the Christian era synchronized with a widely felt need of something to counteract moral deterioration. This created a favorable social atmosphere for Phaedrus and perhaps gave him a stimulus to fasten upon the one Hellenic literary form not yet taken over into Latin; for no claim to be first borrower was any longer open in the field of drama, epic, didactic, elegy, lyric or history. It is characteristic of the period, then, that motifs purely satiric and derived from popular philosophy should enter into the fables of Phaedrus. His own words emphasize his ethical purpose:

> No other aim hath fable in its ken
> Than to correct the errant ways of men.

> (*nec aliud quicquam per fabellas quaeritur*
> *quam corrigatur error ut mortalium.*)[14]

We expect, therefore, to find hits at the same targets as in the διατριβαί, for example, pretentious nobodies or avaricious persons. But Phaedrus does not confine himself to these traditional legacies of theme, nor, though he is unquestionably the Latin Aesop, does he confine himself to Aesop:

> My master's method I shall keep with care;
> Yet, should I please to bring in extra fare,
> So giving pleasure through variety,
> Accept it, reader, pray, with courtesy.[15]

This intention *aliquid interponere* is an essential point to note in justice to the independence of his genius. His outlook on life—always a crucial matter in a satirist—is not fully intelligible unless it is realized that he concerned himself also with social and political conditions in his own age. Fable to him was a convenient literary cloak for an author's real feelings. Within limits, then, it might convey political satire: only, it was concealed and therefore a contrast to the undisguised attacks of a Lucilius. I translate significant lines from the prologue to the third book:

> Now shall I briefly show why this same sort
> Of fable was invented. Slavery,
> In its subjection to another's will,
> Because it dared not utter what it wished,
> Transferred to fables its own sentiments,
> Eluding censure by pretended jests.[16]

He widened its path into a highroad, he proceeds to say in this, the most instructive, of his prologues, bringing misfortune upon himself through the enmity of the once powerful minister, Sejanus. He had thus learned the peril even of veiled satire. Yet his express purpose was to avoid personal attacks:

> My verse will brand no individual,
> But life itself and ways of man display—
> "A heavy task to promise," one will say.[17]

This is virtually the same as Martial's motto, "My page smacks of man,"*hominem pagina nostra sapit*. But a political construction was put upon his King Log and King Water-snake; in the proud Jackdaw some saw Sejanus; and into the threatened wedding of the scorching Sun-God (though this is an Aesopian fable) was read an allusion to one of the ambitious minister's matrimonial schemes. Sometimes, however, there are pieces frankly dealing with Roman life. One[18] is the story of a conceited flute player named Princeps, prominent in the public eye as accompanist to the pantomime-actor Bathyllus, Maecenas' freedman. Returning to the stage on his recovery from an accident which had incapacitated him for some time, he earned ridicule by his impulsive egotism in taking as applied to himself what a chorus sang about the Emperor,"Rejoice, O Rome, secure: thy Prince is well!" He was not the only Princeps in the city. Another piece[19] tells an anecdote about Tiberius intended to deride the *ardaliones* of Rome, those idle busybodies who appeared to have endless time upon their hands, and off whom he scores by oxymora:

> *Ardaliones* are a clan at Rome,
> Panicky hustlers, busy at their ease,
> Panting for naught, fussing with no result,
> Boring themselves and loathed by other folk.
> I'd fain reform them, if I only can,
> By this true story, worth your while to scan.

The story sets forth how once Tiberius, while residing at his country seat on Cape Misenum on his way to Naples, observed a very officious slave at each turn in the garden shrubberies sprinkling the parched ground from a watering pot. He reappeared everywhere until His Majesty grew tired of seeing him, and divined that his object was simply to attract attention and perhaps obtain manumission, indicated by a master's symbolic smack (*alapa*) in the act of liberation:

> "Come here!" the Emperor cried. The knave skipped up,
> Brisk in the joyous hope of sure reward.
> Then His Imperial Highness scored his jest:
> "Your fuss means nothing: all your toil is lost:
> Far more with me the slaps that free men cost."

The charge of pessimism has been alleged against Phaed-drus: his beast world, it is urged, is one where tyranny, cruelty, and guile too often get the upper hand, and where animal nature is painted too "red in tooth and claw." The satirist, however, must always see more vice than virtue in what he attacks; and yet wickedness is not uniformly triumphant in the fables. To take examples from the first book—the vain jackdaw is disgraced, the greedy dog loses the meat he has, the wolf is punished for false witness, the faithful dog unmasks the bribery attempted by a thief, and interested advisers are detected by the discreet.[20] The fabulist, in fact, knew the vicissitudes of fortune too well to be either confirmed pessimist or confirmed optimist:

> Be temperate in glee, nor quick complain;
> For life is but a blend of joy and pain.[21]

Another charge submits that reality is contradicted when, for instance, the swimming, and presumably splashing, dog is supposed to see the piece of meat mirrored in the stream, and that his zoölogy is weak when Phaedrus sends a cow, she-goat, and sheep on a carnivorous expedition with a lion, but in the latter fable three of the allies would learn the meaning of "the lion's share," and there is no need for such meticulous pedantry. The fabulist is not concerned with scientific accuracy; he ignores the laws of natural philosophy and natural history, provided he can convey his lessons.

Nor is Phaedrus always as solemn as some of his critics. With a gift of humor he aimed at providing amusement. Justice Ape on the bench with a wolf as plaintiff and a fox as defendant on a charge of theft, knowing well the character of both parties, and having duly weighed the cross-swearing, pronounces his comical judgment:

> You, Wolf, it seems, ne'er lost what now you claim;
> I hold, glib Fox, you stole it just the same![22]

Judge Wasp is rather less funny in his Solomon-like mode of testing bees and drones as litigants asserting their claim to a store of honey.[23] Public gullibility is pleasantly ridiculed by a king's exposure of the quack doctor who had been a failure as a cobbler: His Majesty asks his Council,

> What arrant fools do you suppose you are
> To trust your lives without a qualm to one
> Whom nobody allowed to shoe his feet?[24]

There is, too, a humorous irony in the unintentional discovery by a burrowing fox of a dragon watching a treasure in a dingy den. The fox politely apologizes for the intrusion, explains that gold is not suited to his mode of life, but he would be interested to know what wages the dragon gets for passing his life in wakefulness and darkness. "Nothing at all," replies the dragon; "this is the work assigned me by almighty Jupiter." "Then you don't take anything for yourself or give to anyone else?" "Such is the will of the fates," is the reply. Then the fox sums up, "Well, I don't want you to get angry, if I speak frankly: a person like you must have been born under the displeasure of the gods."[25] From the tone it might be imagined that the questions in the dialogue came from Menippus poking fun at avarice. There is humor, too, in the story of the scented dogs dispatched as an embassy to Jupiter, though the humor is broad.[26] Racy of the soil, and quite one of the best stories, is that of the peasant who competed in pig-squeaking with a professional ventriloquist.[27] The yokel, to ensure perfect truth to nature, concealed under his clothes a little pig from which surreptitious pinches elicited what he knew to be the real thing. The audience thought otherwise, and preferred the artificial imitation:

> The people yelled the mountebank was far
> More true to life: they had the countryman
> Hustled outside. But from his bosom forth
> He pulls the authentic grunter, and convicts
> Their shameful error by a patent proof:
> "This shows," he cries, "what judges you must be!"

In this story, as in that of the quack, Phaedrus' butt is the gullibility of the public.

One quality of style greatly aids Phaedrus' satiric effect: he is neat and straightforward in expression, employing the *urbanus sermo* in the iambic trimeter of Latin comedy[28] without cumbrous verbosity. It is pleasant to remember that "adding insult to injury" is virtually a quotation from him. That was what the bald man did to his own pate when he missed the mosquito that had stung him and fetched himself a ringing slap—*iniuriae qui addideris contumeliam.*[29]

When we pass from Phaedrus to Persius, we meet a solemn young man in whom no humor was. He was a hot gospeler ardent for the application of Stoicism to life. At least two features common in satire are present in Persius, and range him in the true lineal descent—a critical interest in literary questions which we see at once in his first satire, and a passionate belief in philosophy as a cure for social ills. He would not have been the devoted follower of Horace which he is, had these traits not reappeared in him.

Aulus Persius Flaccus[30] was born at Volaterrae in Etruria in A.D. 34. His father, whom he lost when he was about six, had equestrian rank, and the boy's education at Rome began in A.D. 46. His life,[31] a short one of fewer than twenty-eight years, brought him into contact with teachers and friends who profoundly influenced his genius. Among these were Remmius Palaemon, the distinguished but unprincipled professor of literature; Verginius Flavus, the eminent rhetorician who, with the Stoic Musonius Rufus, was banished by Nero; Caesius Bassus, the lyric poet to whom Persius wrote his sixth satire; and notably the Stoic teacher Cornutus. Through him he made acquaintance with contemporary Greek philosophers and with a famous fellow pupil, the epic poet Lucan, who considered his own writings as only sportive efforts in comparison with the genuine poetry of Persius (*illa esse vera poemata, sua ludos*). To Lucan's uncle, Seneca, he was not attracted; but through the younger Arria he knew the dignified Stoic senator Thrasea, a biographer of Cato, and a man whose seriousness was a standing rebuke to the Emperor Nero. A prevailingly Stoic atmosphere, therefore, enveloped the young poet; but it was in particular from Cornutus, who was not only a Stoic thinker but also a grammarian, a tragic poet, and a commentator on Virgil, that he drew the most invigorating sustenance for his intellect. Persius' affectionate nature prompted his tribute of gratitude to Cornutus in his fifth satire. When a mere youth, he had been welcomed to what he calls Cornutus' "Socratic bosom," and the Stoic rule had been applied to straighten moral twists with so much effect that he feels his friend and tutor had become a great part of his very soul.

The other outstanding influence upon Persius was the literary one of Horace's works. To Horace he owed not merely hints on subject-matter such as the treatment of Stoic paradoxes, but a continuous debt in turns of thought and phraseology. His borrowings are, however, seldom direct echoes: a Horatian phrase is, as it were, turned over and over in Persius' mind until it is elaborated into a recondite allusion.[32] The chief among other literary influences on Persius is that of Lucilius, from whom the opening line of his first satire comes, and on whose fourth book was based the third satire. The scazons introduced by Petronius in the *Satyricon*[33] as a kind of Lucilian imitation lend color to the idea that Lucilius' influence acted upon the so-called *Prologus* in the same meter. He was evidently well read in the older Latin poets. Ennius and Virgil are quoted: there is more than one allusion to

Ennius' alleged dream that Homer's spirit had migrated into himself:[34] and fun is poked at archaizers captured by the antique style of Accius and of Pacuvius, whose tragic *Antiopa* "rested her dolorific heart on tribulations" (*aerumnis cor luctificabile fulta*).[35] Persius' own literary sympathies, indeed, were with a virile kind of Latin poetry, so that he could approve a reasonable amount of archaism in his friend Caesius Bassus,[36] just as old-fashioned Roman ways appealed to him. What particularly roused his antipathy was the effeminate new Alexandrinism prevalent at the Neronian court.[37]

His lost works included a *praetexta* play, a book of travel, and lines on the brave Stoic lady, Arria. Cornutus advised, after Persius' death, that these should not be preserved; and according to Quintilian he made good his title to fame in his single book of satires (*multum et verae gloriae quamvis uno libro Persius meruit*).[38] Persius was a rich man and left, with other legacies, his library to Cornutus, who revised the volume of six satires for its posthumous publication by Caesius Bassus.

The great part sustained by Stoicism in Roman satire is obvious. Lucilius was intimate with it through the Scipionic circle; Horace became increasingly Stoic in sympathy; and Stoicism was to color Juvenal's views on human wishes. But with Persius it was bone and fiber of his being. To him Stoic theory was the panacea for literary decadence and social failings. In the early empire Stoicism, as much a creed as a doctrine, was the faith of the noblest minds among the Roman aristocracy: its followers learned a supreme fortitude in facing sorrows in life or the menace of death. Its eminent exponents in the first century were Seneca and Musonius Rufus, after whom Epictetus bequeathed its influence to Marcus Aurelius on the imperial throne in the Antonine age. At Thrasea's house Persius could have listened to Stoicism expounded by Musonius and Cynicism by Demetrius.[39] Musonius was a great moral force: through his earnest asceticism he appealed to the conscience of his hearers: it was he who in the internecine struggles which followed Nero's death imperiled his life by a well-meant though ill-timed harangue to Flavianists and Vitellianists on the enormity of civil war.[40]

In this Neronian age to which Persius belonged, the contrast was very sharp between the high level reached in the thought of Seneca and the depths of unblushing immorality ascribed by his contemporary Petronius to his realistic creations in the *Satyricon*. The Stoic was a seeker after God: his philosophy was a religion and for him in his most exalted moments to live with "Nature" was also to have communion with deity. Doubtless, theory far excelled practice. Seneca himself, despite his professed disdain for external riches and his insistence on the riches of the soul, was blamed for usurious greed; and if staid philosophers fell short of their professions, ordinary society was little likely to pursue closely the ideals propounded. Yet these ideals had a potency of permeation; and in the lower grades of society there was slowly working the leaven of other religions. Judaism and Christianity had by Nero's time made entry even into elevated households, though Christians underwent persecution from time to time and Jews remained from Horace's day till that of Rutilius Namatianus objects of dislike whose religious thought and history were misunderstood even by an observant Roman like Tacitus.

The age of Persius, then, was one of ferment in religious and moral ideas; and when he expresses his lofty views on prayer in his second satire, it is difficult to say whether he reflects Stoicism solely or has been affected by the doctrines of an imported cult. It is certain that this satire marks a much higher standard than the ancient Roman notion of sacrifice and vow as implying a sort of bargain between the worshiper and a Higher Power; what is not so certain is a decision on whether his religious passages indicate a tendency toward a fresh attitude and a wider conception of duty to God, or simply a rational piety which would be approved by most Roman moralists.

If we contrast, for a moment, Persius with his contemporary and admirer Lucan, we find in the latter a genius, more rhetorical than purely epic, who is influenced, no doubt, by Stoicism,—it could hardly have been otherwise when one remembers his Senecan kinship,—but on whom its influence seems incidental and intermittent. With Persius, on the contrary, satiric poetry had to be written to expound his Stoic convictions. In contrast with the impulsive onslaughts of Juvenal, who obeyed an overmastering force of wrath making it "difficult not to write satire," the satire of Persius was the outcome of calculation. He is as wholeheartedly devoted to the enforcement of Stoic philosophy as Lucretius was on the opposite side, though without perhaps the full devastating intrepidity of the great Epicurean poet. Yet he is sincere, if not so bold, in his evangel: in him it is a philosophic student that speaks; the recluse has become an ardent missioner, faithful to the normal principles of Roman Stoicism. If Seneca was ready to modify strict dogma to suit altered circumstances, Persius, as the disciple of Cornutus, discourses with rigid adherence to Stoic orthodoxy on prayer, temperance, wealth, and vain popularity. For him the one thing needful is liberty of soul (*libertate opus est*, V. 73). Some passages, indeed, sound as if they were actually echoes of Cornutus' lectures, like the exhortation in the third satire to learn what kind of life we are meant to lead, and in the fifth satire the warning against procrastination in discovering the true end of life, together with the excellent sermonette on moral freedom.[41] Persius came to his task fortified by lessons of self-subdual and of high aspiration, mindful of the weary vacuity of soul which accompanies a plenitude of animal pleasure, convinced of the nothingness of the chimeras which haunt worldlings, and therefore never to be allured by the empty mirage of terrestrial pomp. Some may resent a certain priggishness in his apostolic manner of lecturing his day and generation, among its juniors though he was; but there remains this amount of justification for his urgent homilies, that a want of deep philosophical interest was on the whole, and with notable exceptions among Stoic aristocrats, a long-standing senatorial tradition at Rome. So many were indifferent or pleasure-seeking or positively vicious that he could not be described as preaching to the converted.

What most editors give as a prologue of fourteen choliambics is by some regarded as an epilogue (and there is manuscript authority for this) and by others as an entirely independent poem by Persius.[42] At any rate, it is a modest or mock-modest disclaimer of inspiration:

> My lips ne'er quaffed the Pegaseian fount;
> Ne'er dreamed I on the cleft Parnassian mount—

"no," he continued, "I am but a half-brother of the poets' guild (*semipaganus*)"; and, with an ironic whine, he poses as himself forced, or parodies contemporaries who were forced, to write because of poverty—which he certainly was not.

His first satire,[43] which turns on the radical interconnection of intellectual with moral vigor, proves how his literary judgment was colored by Stoic insistence that poetry should be useful. Its best parallel is the letter[44] in which Seneca examines decadence in literature as a mirror of morals. This is Persius' *apologia pro satura sua*, as the fourth satire of Horace's first book was his. He cannot avoid satirizing contemporaries, he explains to an imaginary interlocutor. To parade learning or win renown is not his aim; for applause is no test, as can be gathered from the insincere flattery evoked by the erotic pieces of aristocratic poetasters. The decadent modern style pervading some lines given in illustration is rhetorical rubbish, and time-honored Roman virility revolts from such twaddle. Yet, asks the interlocutor, "Why make yourself unpopular by speaking the truth?" To which Persius retorts, "Were not Lucilius and Horace allowed to arraign men's faults? May I not at least tell my secret? And the secret is (low be it whispered!), *All the world has donkey's ears*! Those who relish the free utterance of the Old Greek Comedy should be my readers, not the idlers and buffoons to whom I gladly leave the fashionable trash of the day."

The four lines, I. 99-102, beginning, "Grim horns they filled with Mimallonean booms," (*torva Mimalloneis implerunt cornua bombis*), which are presented as nerveless stuff, used to be taken as a quotation from Nero.[45] It is generally agreed now that they are Persius' own parodic verses, and that neither in this first satire, nor under the Alcibiades of the fourth, is he hitting directly at the Emperor.

Sending birthday greetings to Macrinus in his second satire, Persius rejoices that Macrinus can pray to the gods aright, unlike the majority of great men, whose secret prayers are too wicked to be uttered aloud. This subject of prayers right and wrong is that afterward treated by Juvenal in his tenth satire, and examples, as in Juvenal, are given of shocking or merely silly petitions. The avaricious guardian, the fond grandmother or aunt, the glutton, and others, pass before us and lead up to the impressive fifteen final lines beginning:

> O souls bowed earthward, void of heavenly spark,
> What boots it into temples to import
> These ways of ours, and judge what gods approve
> By measure of the sinful flesh of man?

At the close comes his doctrine of the spiritual offering that is better than sacrifice:

> Duty to God and man, well blent in soul,
> And unstained inmost thoughts and noble heart
> In honor steeped—these let me to the shrine
> Convey: then humble meal will win me grace.

In the third satire a Stoic friend or tutor summons a wealthy young student, who has overslept, to be up and doing—to exchange a life of sloth and revelry for discipline. A realistic picture gives the setting for this serious call. The bright morning (*clarum mane*) is streaming through the shutters, widening the cracks in the strong light, but the carousers of the previous night snore on till lunchtime, when the shadow crosses the fifth line on the sun dial. The youth, aroused, makes ineffectual attempts to write, blames his pen, blames his ink, and is reproached for his degeneracy. Is he to live a life like Natta (one of Horace's figures)? The punishment of sinners should be an epiphany of Virtue revealed as she is in truth:

Let them see Virtue—pine for Her they've lost.

(*Virtutem videant intabescantque relicta.*)

Surely the student has already learned something from ethics:

You have been schooled to mark what leaves the straight,
The lore of that sage Porch with trousered Medes
Bedaubed—

in allusion to the Ποικίλη Στοά, or colonnade, at Athens in which Zeno and other Stoics taught and which was decorated with paintings, including the Battle of Marathon against the Persians. An exhortation follows, that those who are morally weak must seek a cure for their ailment at its first onset, and that the cure is to study true wisdom:

Learn, wretched ones; the causes know of things,
Know what we are, what life we're born to lead.

Stoicism must instruct us how to take critical turning-points in a career, what is the proper attitude toward wealth and toward desire in general, what limits should be set to the claims of kin and country, what part in the world Providence has summoned a man to play *quem te Deus esse iussit et humana qua parte locatus es in re.*

(71-72)

To ignore instruction is to resemble the invalid who follows
the physician's advice only as far as he likes, and loses his
life through gross indulgence:

> Hence funeral trump, wax-lights: the poor deceased
> Laid on high couch, with unguents coarse besmeared,
> Stretches heels doorward stiff and stark: the corpse
> Is shouldered by the citizens his will
> Gave yesterday the right to freedom's cap;

that is to say, by the slaves emancipated under the terms of
his last testament.

The shortest satire, IV, and the longest, V, are arranged
side by side. The call to seriousness in the third is continued
in the fourth with special reference to statesmanship. The
fourth satire is, however, more suitable for Athens in the
days of Alcibiades, who is addressed as "ward of mighty Peri-
cles." Since young nobles of the Neronian age had no avenue
open toward real statesmanship, this satire has some of the
artificial ring of a stock piece of rhetoric— clever and forc-
ible, but scarcely appropriate to its times. Alcibiades professes to be able to guide the state, though his chief good is
merely the Epicurean one of enjoyment. He has never examined his own soul. The keynote of the satire is the need
for self-knowledge in place of self-gratification. The blind-
ness to one's own defects which accompanies criticism of
other people is illustrated by the notion of the wallet on a
neighbor's back, similar to that in Catullus, Horace, and
Phaedrus:

> How few to plumb their own true nature try;
> Inside their neighbor's bag in front they pry.[46]

Such self-complacent carpers at others might well utter
Burns's prayer:

> O wad some Power the giftie gie us
> To see ourselves as ithers see us!

The longest of Persius' satires, the fifth, opens with a beautiful and affectionate acknowledgment of his debt to his honored teacher, Cornutus. It then elaborates, in contrast with their unity of feeling, a picture of the variety of the pursuits which engross men. The theme and treatments apart from the personal element, resemble the dialogue between Horace and Davus on the doctrine that all men are slaves.[47] A quarter of the way through Persius' satire comes the transition. He and his wise monitor are linked in a close-knit friendship by their common devotion to the true philosophy which secures singleness of heart and harmony of soul, unlike the bewildering diversity of purposes in the world:

> Motley is life: thousand the sorts of men.
> Each has his own desire: life's aims diverge.

> (*Mille hominum species et rerum discolor usus;*
> *Velle suum cuique est, nec voto vivitur uno.*)

The vital need for the individual, and ultimately for society, is freedom, not mere civic freedom symbolized by the stroke of the praetor's rod which marked a slave's manumission, but the freedom which comes from duty understood and life used in accord with reason. Reason will emancipate from the various kinds of slavery enumerated, such as avarice, luxury, and superstition. So, he believes, it will cleanse social life.

The final satire, indited from the Italian Riviera to the poet Bassus at his Sabine home, is rather less of a Stoic homily than the four preceding ones. Persius declares his principle to be the avoidance of either of the two extremes of avaricious parsimony or extravagant spending. One need not save for one's heir, even though he might be angry over generosity lavished on a shipwrecked friend:

> Stretched on the beach himself, and therewithal
> Huge painted gods torn off the stern, and ribs
> Of the maimed vessel in the sea gulls' path.

(iacet ipse in litore et una
ingentes de puppe dei, iamque obvia mergis
costa ratis lacerae.)   (VI. 29-31)

—one of the excellent examples of neat realism in Persius
which prove that, far from being enslaved by a cloistered
bookishness, he could observe actuality and express it.

Even this sketch shows that Persius maintains the tradition of the diatribe when he develops a theme by imagining an
objector whose criticism or argument has to be answered.
His burning, almost proselytizing, passion for Stoic truth
stirred him to a dogmatism from which most Romans were
saved by their scrutiny of dogma and paradox under the
guidance of common sense. There is no light-hearted com-
plaisance with the frivolities of men, but a stern urgency in
his summons to austerity of life. This youthful satirist is
possessed, even obsessed, with the need of being earnest, so
that in him one half of the ancient blend of τὸ σπουδαιογέλοιον seems to have evaporated: the serious remains, the
laughter has gone. But he is so centered on the doctrines
which he has compressed in the handling and rehandling of
his phrases that he forfeits the chance of reaching the ordinary reader by plain statement and thereby lessens his social appeal. He forgets that his own keenness must be less
infectious to others for want of clarity. His inveterate habit
of condensing much of his thought into crabbed obscurity
is well illustrated by Quintilian's anecdote of the rhetorical
instructor who kept pressing his pupil to make his composition harder. Renewed efforts brought the coveted result and
won the master's commendation, "Greatly improved—I
can't follow it myself now!"[48] Presumably, too, the composite nature of his style, reflecting the manifold influences
which acted upon him—comedy, the mime, the diatribe,
Horace, and older Latin poets—tended to make his writing
difficult both for him and for his readers: we are told in the
Vita, what we should expect, "he wrote seldom and slowly"

(*raro et tarde scripsit*). His introduction of Roman slang[49] may lend vigor but does not make him any clearer; and, besides his condensation, there are his abrupt transitions of thought, and the difficulty of separating what should be referred to him from what belongs to an objector in his dialogue. Daniel Heinsius, in his *De Satyra Horatiana Libri Duo*,[50] remarks about Persius that, though he appreciates Horace's joyous gift of playing round a reader's very heartstrings, the young Neronian poet has, in spite of this, himself left us so moody a set of writings that he might be thought to have lived on mustard or delivered his Stoic oracles in the cave of Trophonius! For him to enter what Heinsius calls "the Horatian theater" resembles the arrival of a person in funeral garb at a merry wedding party. It is one of the ironies of literature that it should be possible to say this of an imitator of Horace; but it is not the whole truth. Persius was the master of a distinctive style charged, or rather overcharged, with great thoughts: he has left us many imperishable lines, and might have contented himself with the knowledge that he wrote not for the commonalty but for the elect.

CHAPTER VII

MARTIAL—THE EPIGRAM AS SATIRE

Hominem pagina nostra sapit
MARTIAL X. iv. 10

EPIGRAM cannot be called *satura* in the Roman sense. Martial[1] indeed in one poem clearly implies that *satura* was a different literary genre which he had himself attempted, only to be annoyed by the persistent rivalry of Tucca who imitated him in one field after another[2]—epic, tragedy, lyric, *saturae*, elegies, and epigrams. But the epigram can so obviously be used for satiric purpose, and it can in Martial's hands reflect so much of contemporary life that it is a closely kindred form which calls for notice.

The epigram had already passed through a long history before Martial put his distinctive impress upon it.[3] The Greek ἐπίγραμμα, originally an inscription sepulchral or dedicatory in elegiac verse, had undergone a wide process of evolution since Simonides of Ceos used it to honor the dead Spartan warriors at Thermopylae. It was in time extended to cover a neat summary of an event, reflection, or feeling. When thus its delicacy of polished charm gave utterance to emotion stirred by joy or sadness, friendship, a love affair, a storm, a book, a work of art, or a beautiful scene, it approached the frontiers of lyric poetry. This semilyric value varied with the occasion, and occasions, as we see in the Greek Anthology, were infinite. There was nothing to prevent such occasional poetry from embracing satiric themes—the brevity of form lent itself to satiric effect—and under the head of reflection the epigram could adapt itself to themes such as the Stoic diatribe handled. It is not surprising, then, that points of contact between the philosophic homily and the epigram can be found.[4] A poem by Leonidas of Tarentum in the second century B.C., preserved in the *Anthologia Palatina* (VII. 472), was mentioned in the second chapter as virtually an

elegiac diatribe satirizing the fond hopes of man for whom
the worm waits.

When the epigram passed into Roman hands (and there
were Latin epigrams from Ennius' times), the tendency was,
not indeed wholly to extinguish its poetic quality, but often
to subordinate it to satiric design, and especially to a suspension of the stinging point to the end of the poem, a feature in which Martial showed his mastery. This suspension
of point, though not absent,[5] is much less usual in the Greek
Anthology. Some epigrams of unknown authorship in the
Anthology bear sarcastically upon the comedy of human life,
and very likely go back to a date long anterior to Martial.
But the comparatively small number of such poems which
can be safely placed in time before him make it hard to estimate his debt in the way of suggestion to Greek forerunners.
We cannot date, for instance, the epigram on marriage liken-
ing the man who weds a second time to a shipwrecked mariner trying to sail twice across a dangerous gulf; nor is it certain how far back toward Pythagoras' own time we may put
the jest by a meat-eater on vegetarianism: "*You* weren't the
only one to keep your hands off living things: we do so too.
Who's touching live food, Pythagoras? No, we eat what has
been boiled and roasted and pickled, and there isn't any life
in it then!" Some of the rhetorical means of achieving comic
effect (τὸ γέλοιον) were doubtless learned by Martial from
Greek models. About the influence of one Greek writer upon
him we can be fairly sure. This is Lukillos or Lukillios, whose
Greek epigrams, written in Nero's reign,[6] are partly preserved in the Anthology. From him Martial seems to have
taken his cue for one of many gibes at physicians. The Greek
epigram is to this effect:

> Diophantos in his slumber
>   Dreamed that he his doctor met:
> Diophantos never wakened,
>   Though he wore an amulet;[7]

and I may render Martial's adaptation thus:

> He bathed with us: he made the dinner go:
> And yet our friend was found next morning dead.
> Why such a sudden death?—you'd like to know.
> *He dreamed he saw the doctor by his bed!*[8]

Nor can we assess exactly the amount of satiric suggestion which Martial gained from Latin predecessors. In his prose preface to Book I, apologizing for the outspoken coarseness of expression in his epigrams, he pleads that the example was set him by Catullus, Marsus, Pedo, and Gaetulicus. A poem in Book V requests the curator of the Palatine library to grant his little books a niche "where Pedo, where Marsus, and where Catullus are to be."[9] About Marsus, Pedo, and Gaetulicus we know little compared with what we know about Catullus. Their extant scraps are insignificant.[10] Domitius Marsus and Albinovanus Pedo wrote in Augustan times: to the latter Ovid addressed one of his epistles from Pontus.[11] Cn. Cornelius Lentulus Gaetulicus, a composer of erotic poems, was put to death in A.D. 39 under Caligula: it is uncertain whether the nine epigrams in the Greek Anthology under the name Γαιτουλίκου are by him.

The influence of Catullus, however, is strongly marked on Martial. In the *Spectacula* and fourteen other books, out of 1561 epigrams 1235 are in elegiac meter, 238 in hendecasyllabic, 77 in choliambic, and a few are in iambics and hexameters. It is on Catullus chiefly that the hendecasyllabics and choliambics are based, though Martial, unlike Catullus, restricts the first foot of his hendecasyllabics to a spondee. In his chief verse-form, the elegiac, Martial, though generally a follower of Ovid, yet does not confine his pentameter endings to the Ovidian disyllable, but resembles Catullus in using such endings as *ingenio* and *amicitiae*. And the tone of Catullus acts upon him; for a glance at Catullus shows how he had used all three meters for satiric purpose. In elegiacs[12]

Catullus has poems on scandalous revelations in dialogue
with a door, on the vows of woman written in air and water,
on Caelius Rufus as his supplanter in Lesbia's affections, on
Arrius who had the family failing of aspirating Latin words
wrongly, and lampoons pouring out a stream of invective on
Mamurra, Caesar's *praefectus fabrum*, with which can be
coupled the disdainful lines:

> Caesar, I court no favor in your sight,
> Nor yet to know if you are black or white. (Catull. 93)

Many of his hendecasyllabics[13] resemble Martial in spirit—
banter of a victim of amorous excess, remonstrance to a pil-
ferer of napkins, a chaffing acknowledgment of a Saturnalian
gift of an anthology drawn from dabblers in poetry, abuse
of the needy associates who pounced on him soon after his
arrival in Rome, execration of Volusius' historical poetry,
attacks on the vice of Caesar and Mamurra. In choliambics[14]
there are such subjects as the man of wit unlucky enough to
fancy himself a poet, or Egnatius' incessant grin which bares
his teeth; and in iambics,[15] which Martial uses little, complaints against despicable creatures whom the triumvirate
or Big Three appointed to the best places,—for himself Catullus feels nothing is left but to die,—and a bitter attack on
Julius Caesar's toleration of the gross license of Mamurra.

Roman literary men of succeeding generations kept up the
practice of imitating the neat products of Hellenic epigrammatic skill which had occupied the attention of Catullus and
his circle. It was a fashion among the younger Pliny's associates in Martial's own age, as it had been in the Neronian
age when Petronius wrote.

Among the short poems ascribed to Petronius[16] the elegiac
is used not only for the finest piece in the collection, on "The
Sleepless Lover," but also in some pieces satirically, as in
the scoff at Jewish worship of what is ignorantly termed a
porcinum numen and the gibe at a wife as a *legis onus*:

> A wife, a legal burden, should be loved
> Like revenue; but e'en my revenue
> I should not wish to love forevermore.[17]

But Petronius also uses the hexameter with satiric effect, as in his lines on the betrayal of confidence:

> Sooner will mortals in the mouth hold flame
> Than hide a secret. Whatsoe'er in hall
> You let escape you, river-like flows forth
> And beats in hasty gossip upon towns.[18]

In another hexameter poem, after the natural charms of a country house have been described in contrast with the emptiness of luxurious living, Petronius closes with the satiric *i nunc:*

> Go too now: sell the fleeting hours of life
> For rich repasts. I pray the common end
> May find me here to answer for time spent.[19]

This use of the hexameter has importance in the study of Martial. There are, it is true, only a few poems restricted to the hexameter in his works; but he vigorously defends his right to employ the meter. In VI. 65 one Tucca is supposed to object to the writing of epigrams in continuous hexameters instead of the distich. The piece comes just after a comparatively long hexameter poem of thirty-two lines. But, pleads Martial, such meter is both allowable and usual; and he retorts with the advice:

> Read couplets only, if you like what's short.
> Let's bargain, Tucca, that long epigrams
> By me be written and by you be skipped.

> (*si breviora probas, disticha sola legas.*
> *conveniat nobis ut fas epigrammata longa*
> *sit transire tibi, scribere, Tucca, mihi.*)[20]

This most interesting claim for freedom to use various meters has almost the effect of ranging Martial in the tradition of

satura as the time-honored medley. But the vital thing in
him is not his conformity to any tradition or debt to previous
authors, but his originality. His debts to the past were mainly
debts in technique and phraseology: what was his own was
a creative element with unique qualities which raised him
far above mere imitation to a place among the greatest epi-
grammatists in the world.

M. Valerius Martialis was born about A.D. 40 at Bilbilis
in Spain. Although he claimed Iberian and Celtic blood, his
name Valerius is Roman, and his cognomen signified his birth
on the first of March. His literary education, at which in a
cynical mood he scoffs as foolishly given him by his parents,[21]
fitted him for his career in authorship at Rome, whither he
went in 64. It was natural that his earliest patrons should be
his fellow Spaniards Seneca and his nephew Lucan; but the
eclipse of their fortunes and lives in the Pisonian plot of A.D.
65 threw Martial on a long and often disheartening search
for means of support. Whether his farm at Nomentum was
the gift of Seneca or of Polla, Lucan's widow, is uncertain; we
know, however, that Martial kept up his acquaintance with
Polla and honored the memory of her poet husband as one
of the glories of Spain. Celebrating his anniversary he says:

> Apollo's bard and his almighty birth
>   This day recalls: our rites, kind Muses, see.
> This day earned fame—Lucan it gave to earth,
>   That Baetis-stream might blend with Castaly.[22]

All through years of vicissitude at Rome his thoughts re-
verted to his native country with a nostalgia that partly explains his final departure from the capital: the uncouth
place-names come back to his mind irrepressibly:

> Our homeland names are harsh upon the tongue;
> But we, from Celts and from Iberians sprung,
> Must never blush to cite them in our lines—
> Like "Bilbilis," rich in cruel iron-mines.[23]

It is from Spain that he pictured a hunger march to Rome
by one individual, who turned back from the Mulvian Bridge
without so much as entering the city, the moment he heard
how poor were any prospects from the *sportula* allowance:

> A Spaniard who felt hunger's pain
> Set out to Rome hoping for gain:
> At the Tiber he learned
> That no dole could be earned:
> So he made his way straight home again.[24]

There seems to have been a collection of Martial's juvenile
verses;[25] but his earliest extant publication was the *Liber
Spectaculorum*, a set of thirty-three uninspired pieces in com-
memoration of the opening by Titus of the Flavian Amphi-
theater, popularly called the Colosseum. About four years
afterward he issued his *Xenia* and *Apophoreta*, two books,
nearly all in couplets, written to serve as mottoes for Saturnalian presents. These are usually numbered, out of due order,
as Books XIII and XIV. It is, however, with the twelve
books issued almost yearly from A.D. 86 that we have here
to do. They constitute a wonderful gallery of human types
from the highest to the lowest in Rome, sketched in general
with the utmost brevity but with a realism that testifies to
the author's exact observation of life. In contact, on the one
hand, with the Emperor Domitian and his favorites at court,
he was by straitened circumstances brought at the other
end of the social scale into an environment where he could
study the seediest and neediest of creatures.

Satire, irony, disdain, reproach are provoked by vice, in-
competence, even mere peculiarity; and Martial, while he
paid extravagant homage to the Emperor, could also throw
his words freely and incisively at those countless types of
human wickedness or weakness which predominate among
his epigrams. But, if those types predominate and account
for much of his nauseating coarseness, there do appear in his

pages friends true as well as false, wives faithful as well as unfaithful, poets admirable as well as execrable. Martial had a genuine vein of sentiment and kindliness, which shows itself in his grief over the death of a little slave girl or a slave lad.[26] His interest in children is evident, and when he enjoys, as he does, rural scenery, it is in part because he has imagination to see in it the dancing-places of satyrs, fauns, and nymphs,[27] but also in part because it came as a relief from the foulness of much that fell under his notice in town. So he utters a genuine sigh of melancholy over the fair landscape destroyed by the eruption of Vesuvius.

The few honors conferred upon him—an honorary tribuneship without military service, equestrian rank, and the *ius trium liberorum*—left him as impecunious as before. His patrons, from the Emperor downward, seldom played or paid up to the standard of his expectations. At one time he tenanted a room up three flights of stairs in the most sweltering part of the city.[28] Yet he scored some success in ingratiating himself with the well-to-do, and so gained presents or the dole of the *sportula*, however heart-breaking and time-devouring he felt the social duties of an attentive client had to be.[29] In patronage[30] he believed, as a condition for the production of verse:

> Maecenases will bring us Virgils too
>
> (*sint Maecenates, non derunt, Flacce, Marones*).

Patronage could not be enjoyed without effort and sacrifice on the part of the poet; and undoubtedly at times Rome wearied him. But he passed thirty-four years in the capital, until in A.D. 98 he realized that, with Domitian's death and Nerva's accession, a new age had dawned to which the adulation so fulsome in the eighth book and the coarseness in the eleventh were no longer suitable. Indeed he recants unreservedly the groveling flatteries which could not but offend a truth-loving emperor like Trajan:

> In vain, O Flatteries, ye come to me,
> Wretches with lips outworn in toadying!
> I'll call no man my Lord and God again:
> Now Rome has no more room for such as you.
> Be off! far hence to turban'd Parthia,
> And, like base fawning crawling suppliants,
> Print kisses on the soles of gorgeous Kings.
> Here have we got no "Lord" but "Emperor,"
> The justest senator in all the House,
> Whose guidance from her Stygian home brought back
> Plain rustic Truth in her unscented locks.
> 'Neath such a prince, if thou art wise, beware
> Of uttering, Rome, the words thou didst before.[31]

In keeping with this was Martial's elegiac couplet which the scholiast on Juvenal IV. 38 has preserved:

> *Flavia gens, quantum tibi tertius abstulit heres!*
> *Paene fuit tanti non habuisse duos.*

It satirically apostrophizes the Flavian dynasty: "O Flavian imperial house, how much did your third scion (i.e., Domitian) take away from you! 'Twould nearly have been worth while never to have had the other two emperors" (i.e., Vespasian and Titus). The distich very likely occurred in the lost anthology of the more decent poems from the tenth and eleventh books drawn up for presentation to Nerva.

In X. 96 he says his chief reason for returning to Spain is his inability to face any longer the cost of living in Rome. In the Spain which he had never forgotten, comforts and clothing were cheap. "Here in Rome the hearth is barely warm with its stingy fire: there it shines with a mighty blaze. Here hunger costs much and the market bankrupts you; out there is a table laden with the wealth of its own countryside." Other motives operated; but, the decision once taken, he was indebted to his friend Pliny's generosity for the expense of the journey. Ensconced on land at Bilbilis, gifted to him by

a patroness Marcella, he settled down to rustic ease in com-
pensation for more than thirty years of wakeful bustle, as
he tells Juvenal in lines which picture his fellow satirist restlessly walking in the noisy Subura while he has regained his
Spanish home.[32] Three years passed before his twelfth and
last book was ready. By A.D. 104 he was dead; for Pliny in a
letter of that year records his death, remarking that "he was
a man of talent, subtlety and vigor, who showed in his writing a very great deal of wit and pungency combined with
good nature."[33]

His own attitude to his verses is a changing one. At times
he professes they are but sportive trifles, *ioci* or *nugae* or
lusus; but this is not consistent with two of his well-justified
claims that his poems would live and that they were a mirror of mankind. He never more emphatically illustrates the
nature of the σπουδαιογέλοιον typical of satire than when
he shows keen anxiety that his epigrams should not be mis-
taken for trivial jocularities:

> My aim in epigrams he fails to see
> Who takes them for mere sport and pleasantry.

> (*Nescit, crede mihi, quid sint epigrammata, Flacce,*
> *Qui tantum lusus illa iocosque vocat.*)[34]

He proceeds to argue that mythological tragedies on Tereus
and Thyestes are more of a joke than his writing, which is
free from inflated bombast (*vesica*); and, possibly with a hit
at Statius, he declares that people praise tragedies, but they
read epigrams. Elsewhere he assures us he could write seriously.[35] Indeed he does so in a way that proves this was no
empty pose. He could not have been the student of man that
he was without feeling that there is much in life to sober the
veriest zany. Yet in the main the lighter side had an irresist-
ible attraction for him: the ridiculous and the coarse fur-
nished endless material, and he was more of the clever recorder
than the deep thinker.

No one has better expressed the manifold quality in the epigram than the German poet Klopstock in his lines on its essential character (das Wesen des Epigramms):

> Bald ist das Epigramm ein Pfeil,
>   Trifft mit der Spitze;
> Ist bald ein Schwert,
>   Trifft mit der Schärfe;
> Ist manchmal auch—die Griechen liebten's so—
> Ein klein Gemäld, ein Strahl gesandt
> Zum Brennen nicht, nur zum Erleuchten:

which I may render into English

> At times an epigram shoots arrow-wise
>   Its point—to pierce;
> At other times it wears the saber's guise
>   And slashes fierce:
> Yet it is oft—the Greeks preferred it thus—
>   A picture small,
> A flash not sent to scorch, but luminous
>   On life to fall.[36]

Now when we consider this miscellaneous range and content, we shall not expect everything in Martial to be germane to a survey of satire. Much that shows both his nature and his poetic genius at their best does not strictly come within our present purview, for example, poems whose themes are friendship, mourning, or scenery. Nor need we spend time on his extravagant adulation of Domitian already mentioned or on his indecent pandering to the salacious propensities of some readers. Nevertheless, there is much left which is in the tradition of satire.

First of all, there is the autobiographic element, seen not only in his interpretation of the function of his own poetry, but also in records of events in his career, so that some poems might be entitled *De se*. In this "Icherzählung," as the Germans call it, he has none of the reticence of his friend Juvenal. Like the traditional satirist, Martial is frank about his own troubles, his poverty, discontent with patrons, resentment against envious maligners and so forth. In some moods of open avowal or disavowal he disclaims the personal satire which attacks the sinner rather than the sin; or, again, realizing that invective is often an appeal to vulgar minds and that true satire must, as a criticism of social phenomena, possess an attraction for the cultivated intellect, he emphasizes its function as a mirror of life. His task is to dye his Roman booklets in sprightly wit so that "Life may recognize her own manners as she reads."[37] He knows that, whether jocular or mordant, his poetry has won him fame. Even in the opening piece of his first collective issue of Books I to VII, he says he is known the whole world over for his witty booklets of epigram; in the eleventh book he remarks that "Britain too is said to hum my verse."[38] Confident as he was also of literary immortality, he had yet the humbling reflection that he was no better known than a popular race horse:

> Hendecasyllables have made me known
>   And elegiac verse: abundant fun
> That is not too audacious in its tone
>   Spreads Martial's glory widely 'neath the sun
> Mid clans and peoples. Wherefore envy me?
> A horse has equal notoriety.[39]

In another mood he was frequently conscious of inroads on his time, as in his complaint that good verses may be lost to the world if a poet has to dance attendance on a patron, or in his question how amidst the encroachment upon his leisure made by countless social duties he could hope to write a book.[40]

When he turned his eyes from himself to his environment Martial surveyed a field so vast and varied that we must be content with a limited selection of illustrations of his attitude to what was the same world as Juvenal satirized. As a social critic, and like many of his predecessors, he found material to hand in the wealth and luxury around him. The folly of ostentatious opulence, the riches amassed in low but lucrative callings, the upstart's arrogance and his inevitable *faux pas* appear, as it were, abbreviated, in his epigrams, as they did in Petronius. Here is his grim cure for a glutton enjoying a dish of mushrooms not provided for his guests: may his *boleti* prove as deadly as those with which Agrippina poisoned Claudius:

> What a mad dinner party, where you, Sir, alone
> Are gobbling *champignons* with guests looking on!
> Can I find for such gorging a suitable wish?
> May your mushroom resemble old Claudius' last dish![41]

Another poem asks a spendthrift how he achieved the difficult trick of making the million vanish which a grasping mother left him.[42] His own straits forced him to comment on the unequal distribution of wealth:

> If poor you are, then poor you will remain:
> None but the rich today can riches gain.[43]

Some of his elegiacs are brief homilies on enslavement to appetite. Epigram II. 53, opening "Do you wish to be free?" (*Vis liber fieri?*), recalls the fuller Stoic treatment in passages of Horace and in the fifth satire of Persius. Martial uses the same elegiac meter to drive home the unwisdom of procrastination in ordering life aright. To Julius Martialis, a namesake and one of his closest friends, he preaches the transience of joys, and closes with the reminder:

> "I mean to live" are words no sage should say;
> Too late is life tomorrow—live today.

> (*non est, crede mihi, sapientis dicere "Vivam"*;
> *sera nimis vita est crastina: vive hodie.*)[44]

It is a tempered Epicureanism in keeping with his advice to the man whom, with a Horatian echo of the *Labuntur Anni* ode, he calls Postumus:

You'd live tomorrow? 'Tis too late today—
The wise man, Postumus, lived yesterday.

(cras vives? hodie iam vivere, Postume, serum est:
ille sapit quisquis, Postume, vixit heri.)[45]

The truly enjoyable *life*, the *vera vita*, which he pictures in
hendecasyllables addressed to Martialis, is an existence free
for both of them from social etiquette, and from the forum,
but enriched with leisure for promenades, bookshops, colon-
nades, gardens, or baths:

> Now neither lives his life, alas!
> But sees the good days fleet and pass:
> These are lost days; but their amount
> Is strictly put to our account.
> When knowledge can life's lesson give,
> Why doth one hesitate to live?

The Latin is one of the best known passages in Martial:

> *nunc vivit necuter sibi, bonosque*
> *soles effugere atque abire sentit,*
> *qui nobis pereunt et imputantur.*
> *quisquam vivere cum sciat, moratur?*[46]

This attitude is further illustrated by his enthusiastic hendecasyllabic appreciation of the delightful view across the
Tiber from the estate of Julius Martialis on the Janiculum,[47]
and his rapturous pleasure in the carefree life which the even-
ing of his own career brought him in Spain.

Like Lucilius, he kept a rod in pickle for shams, still more
abundant in the cosmopolitan Rome of the first century. So
he denounces Gellia's theatrically unreal mourning for her
father, or the old fellow who dyes his white hair black, or
the pretended Cynic philosopher who imposes on people by
his counterfeit get-up (*imagine ficta*)—"This is no Cynic:
what is he, then? A dog."[48] It is this element of sham that
incenses him in some of his many jests on doctors; for in-

stance, on Diaulus, "Dr. Double-course," the ex-physician
who, when turned undertaker, had undertaken the same job
as before, and might presumably rival Juvenal's "Dr. Themi-
son" in the number of patients he could kill in a single
autumn.[49] There is the light-fingered physician also who,
when detected in stealing a wine bowl from a sick man, pretends he took it to keep him teetotal and so privately im-
pose "Prohibition":

> There once was a doctor who stole
> From an invalid patient a bowl:
>   When found out, he explained
>   "You fool! You have gained:
> Drop your drink if you want to get whole!"[50]

> (*Clinicus Herodes trullam subduxerat aegro:*
>   *deprensus dixit "Stulte, quid ergo bibis?"*

Similarly, he exposes frauds like the man who had done so
well out of the burning of his house that he was thought to
have fired it himself, a touch which resembles a passage in
the third satire of Juvenal.[51]

Among social customs, dinner parties were, we have noted,
a familiar theme in satire. There are many epigrams on stingy
hosts and their mean devices in serving wine or viands on
selfishly economical lines. The invidious distinction between
the patron's and the guests' dinner in III. 60 is comparable
with the theme of Juvenal's fifth satire. The guests themselves come in for equal sarcasm. The systematic dinner-
hunter is hit off:

> Philo takes oath he never dined at home,
>   And this is no exaggeration:
> Philo is never known to dine at all
>   Unless he hooks an invitation.[52]

Then there is the needy or greedy client who smuggles away
some of the food from the dinner table, and the noisy fellow

whose abusive tongue is sure to lose him invitations—"You can't be both outspoken and a glutton," says Martial.[53] The entire system of *clientela* annoys him. The tyranny of etiquette for him meant boredom versus enjoyment.[54]Attendance at the morning *salutatio* in the patron's mansion and afterward in town was felt to be a burden;[55] at the same time, the epigrammatist wastes little sympathy on the client who gave the lying excuse for nonattendance that he had gout, then bolstered up his falsehood by wearing bandages, and ended with the dramatic irony of getting the genuine ailment.[56]

Calculated legacy-hunting, *captatio*, was another traditional theme in satire. There is plain-speaking in VI. 63, where the rich man, out of gratitude for gifts sent him by a designing toady, has written him down in his will his heir. He is told by Martial that he has been angled for; the gifts had a hook:

> Will he bemoan your death with honest heart?
> Bequeathe him nothing, if you'd make him smart.

Equally candid and cynical are the lines in VIII. 27:

> You're rich, Sir, and you're old; so he
> Who makes you presents constantly
> (If you have brains and wit to see)
> Means "Die, and leave your gear to me!"

Fortune hunters also saw prospects in a *mariage de convenance*. One of them would be willing to marry old Paula, if only she were older and nearer death.[57] Another coolly sees hopes in Maronilla's "churchyard cough":

> There lives a rich maid whom a swain
> To court, win, and marry is fain—
> She doesn't look nice;
> She's as ugly as vice;
> But her death-warrant cough is a gain.

(Petit Gemellus nuptias Maronillae,
 et cupit et instat et precatur et donat.
 adeone pulchra est? immo foedius nil est.
 Quid ergo in illa petitur et placet. Tussit!)[58]

The Latin gives a good example of suspension of point to the close. The *recitationes* or readings from literary works at dinners or in public halls—a great social feature in the Early Empire—afford Martial much scope for sarcasm. He tells the bawler who wears a woolen wrap for his recitation that the ears of his audience need the wool more.[59] This is virtually the attitude of Juvenal, who in his exaggerative fashion pictures the marble pillars in a garden colonnade as cracked by the everlasting reciter (*assiduo ruptae lectore columnae*).

Women, who are attacked with such elaborate ferocity in Juvenal's sixth satire, figure plentifully in Martial. He is not blind to the nobility of the Stoic heroine Arria, who stabbed herself to avoid surviving her husband Paetus, adding what Pliny calls the immortal utterance, *Paete, non dolet.*[60] Martial weaves these last words of hers into a neat quatrain in his first book.[61] Nor does he overlook happy marriages and faithful wives. In this respect, despite the unclean women who soil his pages, he is fairer and less depressing than Juvenal. But he shares Juvenal's hatred of cruelty in a mistress who could punish a slave girl barbarously for a trivial oversight in dressing her owner's hair.[62] He also, if only by innuendo, suggests the expert female poisoner:

> Every lady friend she's had
>   Lycoris to the grave attends:
> So, Fabianus, I'd be glad
>   To see my wife with her make friends.[63]

It sounds unfeeling; but we may put down the lines as purely imaginary. There is no likelihood that Martial ever had a wife: he could speak caustically for those who had.

Sometimes it is nothing more than fashion of which he

makes fun, for example, the trade in the hair of German women, to which he alludes in lines on tresses yellower than those of a Northern blonde:

> I sent you late a Nordic ringlet fair
> To show that *you* have far more golden hair.

> (*Arctoa de gente comam tibi, Lesbia, misi*
> *Ut scires quanto sit tua flava magis.*)[64]

There is, indeed, a good deal of jesting, in the manner of Lukillios' epigrams, on a woman's make-up. The resemblance to Martial will be evident if I cite two of his from the Anthology: "Nicylla, some say you dye your hair, but really you only bought the blackest on the market," and again, "You bought your hair, rouge, honey, wax, and teeth in the market: you could have bought a face at the same expense."[65] So Martial makes play with false hair and false teeth:

> Fabulla swears the hair she buys is hers:
> So it's not perjury that she avers!

and
>   (VI. 13)
> T's teeth are black, but L's are white—and why?
> T. has her own set; L. prefers to buy.

>   (V. 43)

In another epigram his cue is the loss of teeth with a spice of scarcely pleasant realism:

> Your teeth, my lady, numbered, I think, four.
> A cough spat two out, then a cough two more.
> Now you may safely cough your whole life through,
> A third cough hasn't anything to do.

>   (I. 19)

There is a slight affectation of nonchalance in his treatment of the convivial habit of toasting ladies in measures of wine equaling the letters of their name. Having no sweetheart, he satirically invokes the god of slumber:

Here's to Justina—seven measures, the same
As the letters she has; and for Laevia six:
Toast Lycas in five and toast Lyde in four:
Let Ida have three: each damosel's name
Must be reckoned as you the Falernian mix.
    But as none of these ladies is here any more,
    Come, Sleep, and your drowsihead over me pour.[66]

Literary questions uniformly interested the satirists of
Rome. Martial was in touch with the writers of his day, and
names the chief poets with the exception of Statius. He may
be said to have carried on an epigrammatic feud with pla-
giarists and critics of his verses, jealous poetasters and conceited writers. Himself straightforward in his style, he is
scathing in his denunciation of rhetoric and of bombastic
tragedies. His own claim is to be realistic, a portrayer of
man, with a contempt for myths.[67] For a playwright enam-
ored of mythological themes he prescribes Phaethon and
Deucalion, in other words, fire and water, as appropriate for
such work.[68] Anyway, he feels sure that poetry does not pay:
better drop it in favor of the law, is his ironic counsel elsewhere: nearer than Greek haunts of the Muses stands the Roman Forum "and there is the chink of coin" (*illic aera sonant*).[69]
Horace, it may be remembered, remarks in the second book
of the *Epistles* on the absurdity of valuing poetry by its antiquity. To this doctrine Martial subscribes with epigrammatic brevity:

You like no bards, Vacerra, but the old:
    Only dead poets you think poets true!
Pardon, Vacerra—may I make so bold?—
    It's not worth dying to be liked by you.[70]

He was indeed not likely to hold a brief for the past, as his
bent toward realism made him a describer of his own day
and much of its corruption. For his lubricity he offers a rather
stereotyped apology that his poems might be wanton but

his life was clean (*lasciva est nobis pagina, vita proba*).[71] Yet
he claims that his jests are harmless. Addressing Domitian
he says:

> Here is Book Five, Sire, of my sportive fun.
> Can any growl my verse has hurt him? None.

He believes also that his verses are able to amuse as well as
to confer fame.[72] It is the serious purpose to which he also
lays claim that leads him to realize that writing epigrams is
a different thing from making a book,[73] and he shows himself a sound literary critic in his pronouncement that, in order
to live, a book must have indwelling power (*genius*).[74] His
own discerning power of depicting his age makes his epigrams
not a collection of isolated poems, but a work whose unity
lies in the lasting picture which it has given of Roman society
in the latter half of the first century.

On the technical side, the effective use of surprise is the
secret of the force felt in the close of many of Martial's epigrams—the sting in the tail. Surprise, the παρὰ προσδοκίαν
of the Greeks, when well managed is a telling element in comic
literature. Artemus Ward related the anecdote of the young
man who claimed exemption from conscription for military
service "because he was the only son of a widowed mother
who supported him," where the fun depends on the unexpected turn of the last three words. To similar suspension of
point in Martial attention has been already drawn; and this
was a special feature of his influence on English imitators in
the eighteenth century. This after all is partly a structural
matter. It was perhaps a greater thing in the polemic and
satiric type of epigram which was his forte that Martial dis-
pensed with personalities, and under fictitious names raised
his satire to a more general level, exhibiting in witty brevity
his realistic vignettes of humanity. The strength of his originality must always be reckoned with in surveying the sources
from which he drew. On his adaptations he impressed the

stamp of his own genius, so that the copy is made to surpass the original. With the world of contemporary Rome for the object of his satire he departs constantly from any Greek or Latin models which he employs. This is why it is perfectly true that there is only one Martial.

CHAPTER VIII

JUVENAL AND OTHER SATIRISTS

Difficile est saturam non scribere
JUVENAL *Sat.* I. 30

Facit indignatio versum
JUVENAL *Sat.* I. 79

THE WORLD on which Martial and Juvenal[1] fixed their outlook was the same. Both poets were in the main interested in the same social phenomena. They were friends; for it can hardly be doubted that the three surviving poems, all with a streak of indecency, addressed by Martial to a Juvenal were meant for the great satirist of the day.[2] The epithet *facundus*, "eloquent," applied in one of them to Juvenal in A.D. 92, would fit either skill in declamation or forensic ability; and there is some support for this latter alternative in one of Juvenal's own satires.[3] Martial from his quiet retirement in Spain, we saw, pictured Juvenal as still treading the noisy streets of Rome about A.D. 101, and among the unsatisfactory medieval lives of Juvenal there is a statement (for what the testimony is worth) that he returned in old age to Rome and broke his heart over the absence of his fellow poet. Most likely this is an invention fabricated to emphasize their friendship. At any rate, both alike unveil contemporary vice; both are concerned with the same themes and types; and they agree in their attitude toward literature and patronage. But, though they present the same world, they do not present it in the same spirit. Juvenal is angrier than Martial ever was; he is more of a pessimist and misogynist. He lacked the eye for beauty in woman or youth which Martial had, or at least he would not let the eye dwell on what he sadly reflects in the tenth satire was a dangerous possession.[4] Martial was a cooler observer of life, and to stigmatize its faults relied upon a well-directed sting rather than on Juvenal's

[147]

continuous lash. It is the method of the brief poem as against sustained satire. No satire of Juvenal's sixteen, except the incomplete sixteenth, falls below one hundred lines in length: the powerful sixth has between six and seven hundred, and three others, III, X, and XIV, are each over three hundred lines long. Another contrast lies in the different metrical forms employed by Martial in contradistinction to Juvenal's use of the hexameter alone. In him, therefore, we return to the prevalent tradition of the formal *satura* as established by Lucilius and continued by Horace. But Juvenal has imbibed with the epic meter somewhat more of the grand style than Horace cared to use. More Virgilian in his hexameter, Juvenal is also more reticent about his own individuality. This comparative reticence—perhaps attributable to epic tradition, and, in any event, making another difference from Martial—gives reason for regret; for it leaves much in his life a blank.

Into the perplexing inconsistencies of more than a dozen medieval biographies of Juvenal I shall not here enter. As I have indicated elsewhere,[5] they leave us little certainty concerning the details of his life. Inferentially we can place his birth about A.D. 60, and his birthplace at Aquinum, where a now lost inscription connected one Junius Juvenalis, who may be the satirist, with military service in a Dalmatian cohort.[6] If he did so serve, then he possibly was drafted to Britain, which would account for his allusions to the chariot-fighting of Britons, to the forts of the Brigantes in Yorkshire, to the oysters of Rutupiae in Kent, to the British whale, to the short Northern night, and to the idea of engaging a professor of rhetoric for far distant Thule. The lives direct attention to his prolonged practice in declamation, a fairly obvious deduction from his style. If banishment ever befell him for lines offensive in high quarters, it is impossible to decide from conflicting records when or to what country, Egypt or Britain, he was exiled. For us it is of greater importance that he knew Rome well, although rural origin conceivably gave him a keen sympathy with the quiet life of small towns.

We are on surer ground when we examine the internal evidence for dates. The sixteen satires were published in five sets or volumes at different times[7]—the first, I–V; the second, VI alone; the third, VII–IX; the fourth, X–XII; and the fifth, XIII–XVI. The allusion in I. 49-50 to the trial of Marius Priscus in A.D. 100 places the initial set at the beginning of the second century; and from two passages in his final volume we can assign Satire XIII to A.D. 127 and XV to 128.[8] This marks a literary activity of about thirty years. Juvenal's writings suggest that he had known privations; but in later life he owned a farm at Tibur, and could entertain in his house at Rome.[9]

Just as in Horace the fourth and tenth satires of the first book and the first of the second are indispensable aids toward a grasp of his theory of satire, so with Juvenal's first satire. He will write because anger compels him: the world around teems with vice, crime, and abuses: evildoers flourish. Professedly, at least, everything done and felt by man since Deucalion's flood is to provide him with material and make up the gallimaufry (*farrago*) of his writings. He thus throws the meshes of his net wide: and his *quicquid agunt homines* forms a good parallel to Martial's *hominem pagina nostra sapit*. But this universality of theme is limited in Juvenal's practice: the deeds dealt with are mainly misdeeds, and the assertion at the close of the opening satire, perhaps a protective blind, that he is to attack only those who are now safely buried alongside the Flaminian and Latin highroads, does not take us far back in time from the world of the early second century in which he saw so much to reprehend. His description of his work as a *farrago* relates it at once to the old medley, the *satura*. Moreover, he specifically designates his field as that of "the great nursling of Aurunca," meaning Lucilius; and he specifies as "deserving the Venusian lamp," that is, a castigation from Horace, certain glaring examples of ill-gotten gains, culminating in the "boodle-fortune" of Marius Priscus, who was convicted of extortion from his province but allowed to go into comfortable exile retaining the spoil:

> The banished governor drinks from two o'clock,
> Reaping the fruit of deeds which heaven shock.
> You won the verdict, Province, but still weep.

Juvenal's realistic power of making a scene live is unmistakable in this opening satire: the reader can almost hear the battling for places as the queue lines up for the distribution of a patron's *sportula*: "Give the praetor his dole, and the tribune next." "No, the freedman is first." "Yes," he says, "*I'm* first on the scene. Why should I fear to defend my place, though I was born on the Euphrates, as the window-slits in my ears would prove, even if I denied it. But my five shops bring me in the requisite 400,000 sesterces (i.e., for equestrian rank). . . . So then, let tribunes bide their turn."[10] Here, as elsewhere, the dialogue marks one of the dramatic elements in satire.

Three satires, II, VI, and IX, are, because of their unsavory outspokenness, omitted in many editions. But their themes are not unfamiliar in *satura*: they touch on sexual enormities. II is on hypocritical moralists, VI on odious women, and IX on a reprobate's woes. Of these the sixth is a brilliant, but in the Juvenalian manner one-sided, onslaught upon the women of the day. The almost dizzily kaleidoscopic changes in the pictures involve a certain incoherence of construction. Juvenal returns to faults lashed earlier in the satire, such as the capricious cruelty of mistresses to slaves; and there is a lack of proportion when he denounces with equal ferocity incorrigibly immoral women and those whose offense is that they parade their learning by quoting Virgil at a dinner party or have the assurance to correct a friend's slip in grammar or simply talk too much or too deafeningly:

> So full a flood of phrases from her wells
> You'd think of basins banged with clanging bells,

> *verborum tanta cadit vis*
> *tot pariter pelves ac tintinnabula dicas*
> *pulsari,*[11]

where the interwined triple alliteration adds emphasis to the Latin. We all know the type—perpetual talk but no conversation. His indictment of such delinquencies as infidelity, amours with gladiators, avoidance of legitimate motherhood, was no doubt deserved. As it is in the essence of satire to be partial, it was not Juvenal's cue to catalogue the good women of Rome, to whose honorable lives sepulchral inscriptions and Pliny's letters bear testimony. What we lose in the all-round strict historical view we gain in the force of one of the most devastating satires in literature.

The keynote of disillusion underlying Satire IX is expressed in lines 125-129, which may be rendered:

> Canst cure my hours misspent and baffled hopes?
> The trivial span of our sad paltry life
> Hastes like a quick-doomed flow'ret to its end.
> We drink: we call for garlands, perfumes, girls,
> While Age steals on us ere we comprehend.

The third satire, on Rome as a place too dishonest and dangerous to live in, is one of the best-known. On it Dr. Johnson based his adaptation,"London." Umbricius has decided to quit a city where honest poverty could earn no living and where peaceful citizens might easily meet their death by day or night. The scheme is an imaginary farewell spoken to Juvenal while Umbricius stands by the dripping Porta Capena ready to take his way southward to the Bay of Naples along with his household chattels packed on a mule-cart. The attack is energetically directed against the subtle craft

of Greeks and Orientals, against treacherous philosophers,
the worship of riches, the dangers from tumbledown proper-
ties or from conflagration or from street accidents or bullies
at night. The dramatic force pervading these three hundred
and twenty-two lines creates unforgettable pictures of the
imperial capital in phrases which come back to the mind:

> *non possum ferre, Quirites,*
> *Graecam urbem,*

> I can't stand Rome made Greek, my citizens: . . .
> Teacher, professor, painter, geometrician,
> Masseur, ropewalker, augur, mage, physician,
> All kinds of trade our starveling Greeklet knows:
> You bid him go to heaven, to heaven he goes.

Johnson, who changed the "starveling Greeklet" to "fasting
Mounseer," also changed "heaven" to another locality.

Take again the incident of fire which has broken out in a
Roman tenement house of the sort usual in the blocks (*in-
sulae*) of buildings to be seen in the restorations at Ostia:

> The groundfloor tenant shouts for "Water!" now,
> And shifts his shabby gear to safety now,
> Three storeys up the smoke now threatens you;
> But you are unaware; for if the alarm
> Starts at the bottom of the stairs, the last
> To burn will be the man whose one defense
> Against the rain is in the tilèd roof
> Aloft, where gentle ringdoves lay their eggs.[12]

Here the observant eye for actual detail is what no practice
in declamation could have taught Juvenal; but he is rhetorical enough to help his realism by the device of alliteration.
Condensed dramatic power, true to the ancient *satura*, characterizes the three brief scenes recording a street accident,
and those representing a respectable citizen in the hands of
a drunken Mohock at night.

Satire IV and, still more, Satire V continue the culinary

element usual in *satura*. Satire IV, after stigmatizing the exorbitant price of 6000 sesterces paid by a rich freedman for a mullet, turns with a mock-heroic invocation of the Muse Calliope to narrate the story of an enormous turbot brought by a fisherman to Domitian's villa at Alba Longa. It was clearly written after Domitian's murder in 96; for allusion is made to the Emperor's death, and the occasion is described in terms too uncomplimentary for publication when he was yet reigning:

> While the last Flavian gashed a fainting world
> And Rome beneath a bald-head Nero cringed.[13]

This forms a parallel to Martial's epigram after Nerva's accession mentioned in the preceding chapter. A Privy Council is summoned to consider the problem of getting a platter big enough for such a fish; and Juvenal's gift of succinct description puts vividly before us the figures of an Imperial Cabinet living under the perilous shadow of Domitian's suspicious caprice. Among them were old and happy-looking Vibius Crispus, as mild a man as ever prosecuted for treason; Pompeius, another informer, ruthless in slitting a throat with a quiet whisper; Montanus, one great unwieldy paunch (*abdomine tardus*); Crispinus, reeking of perfume, about enough to scent a couple of funerals; along with Rubrius Gallus, a man of evil antecedents and, Juvenal remarks, "more brazen than a reprobate writing satire." The phrase *improbior saturam scribente cinaedo*, which was cited in the first chapter, is significant of the moral aim which Juvenal implicitly ascribes to *satura*—the profligate, he felt, had no right to turn preacher: satirizing involved obligations.

Satire V is on the shabby entertainment of clients by patrons of the type of Virro, who feasts on the best and insults his dependents with inferior fare. This theme is a familiar one in Martial.[14] The clients' case is put for them: "All we ask is that you dine with us on equal terms, as citizen with citizen (*civiliter*)."[15] But the humiliating reminder comes that Virro is not prompted by economy: "His aim is to give you pain; for what comedy, what farce (*mimus*) is funnier than a client's gluttony in mourning (for want of a good dinner)? . . . He shows sense in treating you like this. If you can stand every insult, you deserve all you get."[16] But where, inquires Juvenal, where are the patrons of the past? (*Quis tibi Maecenas?*)

In VIII, opening "What matter family-trees?" (*stemmata quid faciunt?*), Juvenal scoffs at the claims of high descent. A Stoic note appears in the contention that virtue, that is, honorable action, not a long pedigree, ennobles a man. By merit, many persons meanly born have risen to true greatness; on the other hand, insolence based on exalted origin marks degeneracy: "hold it the worst of sins to set the breath of life before honor, and lose for living's sake the very grounds of life,"

> *summum crede nefas animam praeferre pudori*
> *et propter vitam vivendi perdere causas.*[17]

The satire ends with the sarcasm that the most ancient Roman pedigrees go back to the sanctuary of Romulus for runaways and malefactors. The first dwellers in the newly founded city were plain peasants or—well, persons Juvenal would rather not characterize (*aut pastor fuit aut—illud quod dicere nolo*). It is a humbling thought for snobs.

With X, on "The Vanity of Human Wishes," we reach the first poem of Juvenal's fourth book and of his more reflective satires—pieces in that quieter spirit which prompted Ribbeck's theory of dual authorship in *Der echte und der unechte Juvenal*. No one now seriously believes that the change is more than a gradual evolution in the author comparable to that in Horace himself, in Tacitus, and, to cite English examples, in Carlyle and Browning. In these remaining satires there is a mass of noble thought, even if the former

violence of indignation has gone. Dryden's argument to the
tenth calls it "this divine Satyr," and it preserves a permanent classic appeal in its exposition of the various vain prayers
of man and their folly. Containing as many lines as a leap
year has days, it is Juvenal's second longest. I refrain from
any analysis of its instances of the hankering after political
power, oratorical fame, military glory, length of life, beauty
of person, and content myself with a translation[18] of his close
on a Stoic note:

> So shall men pray for naught? If you desire
> Advice, you'll trust the gods themselves to give
> What most befits us and fulfills our needs.
> The gods will grant, not joys, but what is best.
> They love man more than man loves self. Inspired
> By feelings and the power of blind desire,
> We crave for wife and offspring; but heaven alone
> Knows what the children or the wife will be.
> Yet that you may ask something, and pay vows
> At shrines with victims' inwards, offering
> Prophetic cutlets of a pigling white,
> Pray for a sound mind, in a body sound,
> Ask for a valiant heart that death defies,
> That counts life's close as Nature's final boon,
> Able to bear whate'er of travail comes,
> Stranger to wrath, free from desire, convinced
> That Hercules's woes and cruel toils
> Outrival amours, feasts, and Eastern couch.
> I show what you can give yourself. The path
> To tranquil life is Virtue's path alone.
>   Thy power, O Chance, is lost, if men be wise:
>   *We* make thee Goddess, thronèd in the skies.

Here the Stoic insistence on Virtue is clinched by the defiance
of the Epicurean *Fortuna* in the last couplet. The one jocular line in a serious passage ("prophetic mincemeat of a little
white pig," *exta et candiduli divina tomacula porci*) introduces
the laughable ingredient in the σπουδαιογέλοιον. But why?

It cannot mean that Juvenal intends flippantly to mock his own counsel. More probably, like Persius at the end of his second satire, he lays no stress on the mere sacrificial offering: the victim is trivial in comparison with the spirit which accompanies the prayer.

Satire XI, on the characteristic Horatian themes of extravagance and simplicity, falls into two parts, of which the first, about a quarter of the whole, condemns the gourmand who feasts immoderately, neglectful of the heaven-sent maxim "Know thyself," and the remainder is an invitation from the poet asking a friend, Persicus, to an enjoyable but unpretentious meal. A personal touch indicates that Juvenal is now an old man:

> Let my shrivelled skin,
> With gown discarded, drink spring sunshine in.[19]

The occasion of XII is Juvenal's delight over the escape of another friend, Corvinus, from shipwreck. In honest gratitude to the gods he is to offer sacrifice. His motive is piety, not any desire to curry favor with his friend and to be mentioned in his will. This affords a transition to a common theme of satirists—legacy hunting. As his friend has three little heirs, Juvenal observes scathingly that nobody would squander a dying hen on so profitless a family man; but if rich childless people catch a fever, persons come forward with vows of a hundred oxen—big victims are essential for the sacrifice—unfortunately, elephants are unavailable in Rome!

The fundamental purpose of XIII is to console Calvinus, who has been defrauded by a false friend, with the doctrine that vengeance belongs to the gods and heaven will repay. Punishment comes from a remorseful conscience:

> Vengeance must ever please the petty mind,
> Puny and weak. Take this as proved, because
> None more than woman dotes upon revenge,[20]

where his corollary accords with the misogynism expressed in the sixth satire.

Parental example is the main theme of XIV, and its preaching of morality has much of the Horatian ring. Its principle is inherent in the maxim:

The child deserves the utmost reverence

(*Maxima debetur puero reverentia*).

A bad home may teach evil habits like gambling, gluttony, cruelty, and lewdness. From his general theme of domestic example Juvenal turns after line 106 to concentrate chiefly on avarice in the remaining two-thirds of this long satire.

Satire XV illustrates Egyptian barbarity, cannibalism indeed, from the feud between two villages; and XVI, dilates on unfair advantages which soldiers possess over civilians.

Juvenal fulfills one of the primary functions of great satire in the portrayal of his times. Taken with the requisite allowance for the censorious attitude inherent in satire and for the special Juvenalian tendency toward exaggeration, he is a valuable index, comprehensive though not complete, to the society of imperial days, its grades, and its usages. We must expect to meet mainly censurable persons in his pages; for a satirist finds little material among the truly good. As a corrective for Juvenal's angry pessimism we have, as indicated in another context, the testimony of Pliny's letters, as well as inscriptions, to a different side of the contemporary world, which shows countless examples of happy and contented lives and of generosity, fidelity, attention to duty, honesty, purity, and affection with other virtues both public and private.

There is a marvelous range in his figures, from a Privy Council at Domitian's court down to the shivering slave to whom a gambling patrician master would hardly allow a tunic once a year, or the wretched beggar graphically described as running beside coaches along the Appian Way, and, in the hope of getting a coin, blowing his wheedling kisses to the occupants.[21]

At the top of the social scale are the nobles, blameworthy in Juvenal's eyes, perhaps most of all for two reasons: they fell short both of the historical standard of the ancient nobility which he revered, and of the ethical standard which he set up. He is horrified at the monstrosity of a noble fighting in the arena or acting on the comic stage; he is disgusted with an audience "that can survey the triple-dyed buffooneries of patricians, that can listen to a Fabius barefooted in a mime."[22] What, he asks, would old-fashioned Romans, a Curius, the two Scipios, Fabricius, or the shade of Camillus think of the degenerates of modern times?[23] His ethical standard for the upper classes is that of Persius.[24] Mere inheritance of ancient lineage is worthless: *noblesse oblige*. The obligation according to Persius is to be up and doing, to renounce slackness and vice. The obligation according to Juvenal is to act nobly—noble is he who nobly acts (*nobilitas sola est et unica virtus*): "You must be a Paulus or a Cossus or a Drusus in character": no one would call an animal high-bred if it proved degenerate.[25] If he notes impoverished scions of nobility who have fallen on evil days, like a Corvinus in service on a pasture-farm, it is rather against the luxury and insolence of self-indulgent nobles that Juvenal's ire is roused —lavish in spending on themselves, but stingy to clients and loth to give practical help to needy poets. From among their ranks too there came, under the worst emperors, informers enriched by unscrupulous prosecutions for treason; and so Juvenal leads up to the spies attending Domitian's council in the fourth satire by his introduction concerning the fisherman who caught the prodigiously large turbot. He did not dare to sell it: it would have been a deadly peril to withhold it from His Imperial Majesty in days "when even the seashores are thick with informers" (*cum plena et litora multo delatore forent*).[26]

On the next grade, the *equites*, Juvenal, like Martial, has much to say, particularly with regard to the coveted *census* of 400,000 sesterces, the shady ways and mean occupations whereby the qualifying money was obtained, the admission to the special equestrian rows in the theater, and the right to wear the ring of knighthood, sometimes impudently assumed by impostors.

For the plebeians, keen on two things only, the corn dole and free amusements (*panem et circenses*, in Juvenal's immortal phrase),[27] he feels considerable contempt, tempered with a fellow feeling for their poverty,[28] and pity for the miserable pittance which was their main source of subsistence, of clothing, and of firing at home (*quibus hinc toga, calceus hinc est et panis fumusque domi*).[29] Persius had testified for the Neronian age that "any Publius enrolled in the Veline tribe becomes possessed of a ticket for a ration of mangy corn."[30] Politically the ordinary citizens no longer counted for anything: they had now lost the right even to sell their votes (the satirist speaks).[31] Socially too they seemed negligible, if they could tamely submit to the supercilious contumely of a patron and his slaves.

Slaves are presented vividly to our notice. They were of undeniable importance because of their numbers and their constant addition to the freedman class through manumission, with the consequent copious transfusion or infiltration of alien blood into the citizen body.[32] They were of very different nationality and of very different abilities, physical and intellectual. The ordinary household slave is the commonest type in Juvenal; for example, the six strapping bearers to carry a *lectica*, the attendants to escort the master home by the glare of torchlight in contrast with the scanty candle or moonshine on which a poor citizen had to depend; the active domestics preparing a bath for their owner on his expected return; or pampered lackeys who might, unless bribed, deny to a client the chance of calling on a patron.[33] Some slaves were attractive for their accomplishments or looks, often in fact bought for their good looks; but others were unprepossessing, like the repulsive blackamoor who waited on the seedy clients at Virro's dinner, "one whom you wouldn't like to meet at dead of night (*cui per mediam nolis occurrere noctem*) as you're driving past the tombs on the Latin Road."[34]

But the man who had been brought to Rome "with whitened feet" (i.e., marked "For Sale") frequently saved enough *peculium* to buy his liberty, or received it by emancipation in his master's lifetime or after his death. For such of this freedman class as accumulated wealth Juvenal has a dislike so intense that it is difficult to credit the medieval biographical statement that he was a freedman's son. The statement may be an ill-considered echo of what was fact in the case of Horace.

To some of the social usages common in the period, such as the *salutatio* by clients and the *recitatio* by authors either at dinners or in halls, allusion has been made. In passing, attention should be directed to the admirably full but not stereotyped menu at Virro's banquet.

Equally graphic are his references to external conditions —the bustle and danger of the streets, the tottering state of some of the house property in Rome, and the dingy hovels occupied by the poor. Such pictures make a realistic setting for what most concerns him, the life of the times and its faults which demanded castigation.

Indignatio facit versum, says Juvenal:[35] "Wrath is the maker of my verse." The author ought to know whence his main inspiration comes; and the thunder of explosive anger is abundantly audible in the earlier books. Yet there is a sense in which this familiar quotation tells only part of the truth. People can be immeasurably angry without achieving the satiric; for anger, to rise above mere invective into satire, must be artistically directed; and this is where Juvenal's own talents are necessary for the complete recipe. He knew how to direct his anger so as to hold up the mirror to a degenerate Rome and, in Hamlet's words,"show scorn her own image." That he is given to overstatement is no proof of insincerity. Abuses, he felt, existed plentifully and justified reprobation even in unbridled terms. His colors may be too dark, but he does not victimize the innocent. It is of the essence of satire to select its subjects for attack, and when, he asks, was any age richer in material? If he lets virtue and merit pass unrecorded, though at any rate unassailed, it should be borne in mind, as already suggested, that it is not a satirist's business to present a complete view of contemporary society. He wields a scourge from which goodness is exempt. Juvenal may be called "a good hater," but it is the sin rather than the sinner that earns his passionate hatred. This relative impersonality sublimates a hatred which, when justifiably evoked, brands an abuse as blameworthy morally and socially. That is the indignation which makes satire a salutary medicine. In its administration Juvenal takes himself seriously. His attitude to vice, in his robust and fiery denunciation, is totally different from that of Petronius, whose portrayal is the product of a mind seared by pleasure to a cynical callousness. This denunciation also differentiates him from Horace, who in his mellower years grew more and more compassionate toward human faults. Juvenal's pungent ferocity is comparable rather with the remorselessness of Swift; yet between these two there is a contrast. Swift's savage misanthropy, partly traceable to disappointed ambition which deprived him of a social influence commensurate with his talents, was exhibited more strongly in his later writings, whereas the quieter tone of Juvenal's later satires marks his departure from the old *saeva indignatio*.

Juvenal doubtless employed rhetorical commonplaces and artifices freely. Rhetoric had taught him how to secure effect, how to multiply instances, even how to intensify indigna-

tion. Whether the Stoicism in him came entirely from academic commonplaces (*loci communes*) or partly from reading such philosophers as Seneca, is a debatable question;[36]
but the literary point of importance lies in the masterly use
of his resources whencesoever drawn. No training in a rhetorical academy and no practice in declamation could guarantee the production of a Juvenal. A genius is not made by
materials, but knows better than others how to control them.
It is true that the *controversiae* recorded in the elder Seneca's
collection took occasion to assail the vices of men and women;
but it does not follow that at every turn Juvenal's inspiration came from *declamationes*. Vices did exist around him:
he could use his eyes.[37]

It is intelligible that Juvenal's forceful rhetoric should
have led some to suspect under his brilliancy a want of truth
to actuality; but how much exaggeration constitutes falsehood is a problem susceptible of different answers. There is
more likelihood of agreement concerning his lack of that un-
constrained ease which is one of the charms of Horace's *sermones*. Even so, lines and phrases of his, simple and straightforward, abide in the general memory and rival the most
familiar things in Virgil and Horace, such as *mens sana in
corpore sano; probitas laudatur et alget; hoc volo, sic iubeo, stat
pro ratione voluntas;* or *occidit miseros crambe repetita magis-
tros.*

With humor some have refused to credit him. Yet it seems
impossible to read through Juvenal with never a smile. Sometimes his humor takes the form of hyperbole, a type well
understood in America, as may be illustrated from Mark
Twain's advice to a young consultant about the proper amount
of fish diet suitable as a stimulus to brain power. Judging by
a specimen of literary composition submitted, Mark Twain
suggested that a couple of whales might meet the case. A
Juvenalian parallel is the suggestion already mentioned that
the person ready to sacrifice a hundred oxen to ingratiate

himself with a rich and childless man might instead have
used elephants—only, they were unobtainable at Rome! Anti-
climax is another factor in his humor—that is, an exaggerated seriousness or comic emphasis is attached to the last
member of an ascending scale. Could any horror be worse,
he asks in the third satire, than "conflagrations, the incessant
falls of buildings, the thousand dangers of the cruel city, and"
—apparently worst of all—"poets reading out their verses
in the hot month of August?" Usually grim, it is a humor
exemplified in such a scene as that of the hapless citizen en-
treating a bully at night for permission to go home with just
a few teeth left. Some of his allusions, too, are amusing: to
substitute for "Pluto" the circumlocution "Ceres' son-in-
law" has the underlying jest that this was what Proserpina's
distressed mother, Ceres, never wanted him to be. And perhaps one should not read with absolute solemnity a question
like *Quis custodiet ipsos custodes?* "Who's going to mount
guard over the guardians themselves?" This rather mordant
humor adds to Juvenal's appeal, because it marks ability to
relax his prevailing seriousness. Without some such relaxation of intensity he would have been far more circumscribed
in his view of life.

Juvenal's strength lay in employing his verbal armory for
indignant attack upon faults deserving censure, not on superficial things in the manner of decadent satirists. A satirist
who is to live does not waste his force upon merely transient
foibles. His best work must be universal. So great satire does
not die. It transcends the limits of its own period in virtue
of its truth to human nature. Themes like money and sex,
which are among the most constant objects of satire, are as
vital today as they were for Stoic preachers or Roman satirists. Thus satire achieves a classic permanence of appeal.
That is why we read Horace and Juvenal, and that is why
we quote them. Their words are still as true to life as they
ever were.

A sketch of minor satirists in the classical age is histor-
ically justifiable—not so much for the sake of the mere catalogue as to show that satire was cultivated by others besides
the great writers whose works have survived in whole or in
part. The brief allusion made by Horace[38] to Varro of Atax
(82-37 B.C.) leaves enigmatic the nature of the unsuccessful
contribution made by him and several others (*quibusdam
aliis*). Among these others may have been L. Abuccius or
Albutius, who died apparently before 54 B.C., and produced
writings, Varro says, "of a Lucilian stamp" (*Luciliano char-
actere*);[39] and C. Trebonius, Caesar's legate in Gaul, who was
the author of *versiculi* and gratified Cicero by making a collection of his witty remarks. Sevius Nicanor, a freedman,
who was a learned teacher, composed, according to Suetonius,[40] a type of satire characterized by what we may call the
Lucilian trait of self-portraiture. Another freedman, Lenaeus,
from affection for his patron Pompey's memory, delivered
a violent attack on the historian Sallust.[41] Most, perhaps all,
of these inherited a Lucilian strain.

In Horace's own period, his junior friend Julius Florus,
to whom he addressed Epistles I. iii and II. ii, based his satires, according to Porphyrion, on Ennius, Lucilius, and
Varro. In the Silver Age, we have seen that two main streams
of satiric tradition flowed, the Menippeo-Varronian followed
by Seneca and Petronius, and the Luciliano-Horatian followed by Persius and Juvenal. With the former, the Menippean, and therefore alongside the *Apocolocyntosis*, we should
perhaps class the lost *Resurrection of Fools* (μωρῶν ἐπανάσ-
τασις) intended, Suetonius records,[42] to ridicule the idea that
Claudius acted the fool under Caligula to save his life—he
was fool enough without any pretense.

Nero himself wrote satiric verse and was in turn satirized.
We had occasion in the fifth chapter to mention his satiric
bent, as shown in writings which have not survived, namely,
his verses attacking Afranius Quintianus, and his "One-

eyed Man" directed against Clodius Pollio, a man of prae-
torian rank. In Tacitus we read of slanderous verses against
the Emperor (*probrosa adversus principem carmina*) recited
on a festal occasion by Antistius (Sosianus) in A.D. 62, and
we read of Curtius Montanus as the author of similar *carmina* in A.D. 66.[43] In Statius' time, Manlius Vopiscus composed satires as well as lyric, epic, and epistolary poetry.[44]
If in Martial X. 99 *saturis* is correctly read for *satyris*, then
Julius Rufus was a contemporary satirist; and, if Friedländer's explanation of this epigram is right, there were editions
of his work with a portrait as ugly as Socrates. To the same
period belongs Turnus, who, as mentioned in the first chapter, devoted his intellectual powers to satire (*contulit ad
saturas ingentia pectora Turnus*) because he did not wish
to rival his brother in tragedy.[45] Rutilius Namatianus in the
fifth century couples his name with Juvenal's, declaring that
Lucillus, father of Decius, *consularis Tusciae*, equaled both
in satire. Juvenal mentions an otherwise unknown Cluvienus,[46]
perhaps sarcastically, as writing verses like his own, and
Valla's scholion on Juvenal I. 20 refers to one Silius as a satirist of the day. He may be identical with Silius Proculus,
who sent poems to the younger Pliny for his opinion.[47] Sulpicia's so-called satire in seventy hexameters on Domitian's
reign is too late in meter and style to be justly ascribed to
the Sulpicia, wife of Calenus, who wrote love poems in Pliny's
time.[48]

Satire later than Juvenal does not here directly concern
us beyond a brief indication of its continuance. It has been
made the subject of a study by A. H. Weston.[49] Some satiric
elements are incidental, like Namatianus' scathing references
to Jews and Christians in his *De Reditu*.[50] Others appear in
separate attacks, like Claudian's hexameter invectives against
Rufinus and Eutropius, who were ministers of the Eastern
Emperor Arcadius. Christian apologetics gave openings for
satiric writing in prose: of this a good example is Tertul-

lian's *De Pallio*. The parodic side appears in the imaginary will by a pig, *Testamentum Porcelli*, mentioned by Jerome and given at the end of Buecheler's edition of Petronius.

It would take us too far afield to do more than note the influence of Martial's hendecasyllabics on neo-Latin poets, or the survival of the Menippean form, already recorded, in the hands of Lipsius and Cunaeus. A significant collection of Varronian and other Latin prose satires, often on literary themes, was issued at Leyden in 1655.[51]

Satire thus had a long existence in Latin. But its most powerful achievements were attained in the strictly classical age, which admirably illustrates in its great masters the different types of authors who lift their voices not in harmony with contemporary life, but in protest more or less genial, and who, according to temperament, angrily impeach or sagely instruct or cleverly ridicule their times. In this book, stress has been laid upon the social outlook and social value of satire—its pictures of the varied sorts of men and women who constitute a society, its jests, its exposures, its lessons and admonitions. Though the satirist's accents, whether of resonant invective or diverting laughter, do not always appear to ring in unison with the environment which stirs him, he would fain, if there be power in his literary work, stimulate his less sensitive fellow men toward an ultimate harmony achievable through a salutary change in modes, in manners, and in morality.

NOTES

(1) It would be incorrect to say absolutely that satire is no longer written as a separate form, in view of Mr. Sassoon's satiric poetry and the free-verse satires of Mr. Sitwell. More recently, in 1934, "The Bubble," by Mr. Gerald Bullett, was a clever skit in Popian couplets on publicity in connection with fiction, and Mr. Robert Nichols' "Fisbo" ridiculed a literary charlatan.

(2) Isaac Casaubon, *De Satyrica Graecorum Poesi et Romanorum Satira Libri Duo* (Paris, 1605; Italian translation by A. M. Salvini, Florence, 1728).

(3) Juv. XV. 131 sqq.

(4) Sen. *Contr.* I. vii. 13, *hunc sensum cum postero die declamaret in ironiam vertit.*

(5) First published in 1878; later included in Nettleship's *Lectures and Essays*, 2d ser. (Oxford, 1895).

(6) See B. L. Ullman, "Satura and Satire," *Class. Philol.*, VIII (1913): 173-194, and "The Present Status of the Satura Question," Univ. of No. Carolina *Studies in Philol.*, XVII (1920): 379-401.

(7) Keil, *Gramm. Lat.* (1857), I: 485.

(8) Ullman criticizes this widely accepted explanation by pointing out that Diomedes' examples here illustrate *lanx*, not *satura*.

(9) A. Dieterich, *Pulcinella* (Leipzig, 1897), pp. 75-77.

(10) A. L. Wheeler, "Satura as a Generic Term," *Class Philol.*, VII (1912): 457-477.

(11) Nonius 474, 22.

(12) *De Gramm.* ii.

(13) Gellius *N. A.* II. xviii.

(14) Juv. III. 321 sq.

(15) Juv. I. 30; IV. 106; VI. 634.

(16) Juv. I. 30.

(17) Tac. *Ann.* XV. 49.

(18) Juv. VI. 634-637.

(19) J. D. Duff, *Juvenalis Saturae XIV* (Cambridge, 1900), Introd., p. xxxiii.

(20) E.g., *Inst. Or.* IX. ii. 36, *in satura tradit Ennius.*

(21) *Inst. Or.* X. i. 93-95.

(22) In Martial X. 99 it is doubtful whether the true reading is *in saturis*, "in satires," or *in Satyris*, "among a group of Satyrs."

(23) Val. Max. II. iv. 4, *paulatim deinde ludicra ars ad saturarum modos perrepsit.*

(24) *Hermes*, II: 225-226.

(25) F. Leo, "Varro und die Satire," *Hermes*, XXIV (1889): 67-84; *idem.*, "Livius und Horaz über die Vorgeschichte des römischen Dramas,"*ibid.*, XXXIV (1904): 63-77; G. L. Hendrickson, "The Dramatic Satura and the Old Comedy at Rome," *Amer. Jour. Philol.*, XV (1894): 1-30; *idem*, "A Pre-Varronian Chapter of Roman Literary History,"*ibid.*, XIX (1898): 285-311.

(26) C. Knapp, "The Skeptical Assault on the Roman Tradition Concerning the Dramatic Satura," *Amer. Jour. Philol.*, XXXIII (1912): 125-148; R. H. Webb, "On the Origin of Roman Satire,"*Class.Philol.*, VII (1912): 177-189; B. L. Ullman, "Satura and Satire," *ibid.*, VIII (1913): 172-194; *idem.*, "The Present Status of the Satura Question,"

Univ. of No. Carolina *Studies in Philol.*, XVII (1920): 379-401. The theories of Leo and Hendrickson were not accepted by F. de Paola in *Le origini della satira Romana* (Citta di Castello, 1909), nor by P. Lejay in his edition of Horace's *Satires* (Paris, 1911).

(27) See J. Wight Duff, *A Literary History of Rome to the Close of the Golden Age* (1909), p. 642. Livy began writing his history about 27 B.C. He had gone as far as Bk. IX. xviii. 9 before 20 B.C., as, when he wrote that, he did not know of the recovery of Roman standards from the Parthians in that year.

(28) H. M. Hopkins, "Dramatic Satura in Relation to Book Satura and the Fabula Togata," *Proc. Amer. Philol. Soc.*, XXXI (1900): 1-51.

(29) *Inst. Or.* X. i. 93.

(30) Hor. *Sat.* I. iv. 1-8.

(31) See G. L. Hendrickson, "Satura tota nostra est," *Class. Philol.*, XXII (1927): 46-60.

(32) This is Professor W. Rennie's view, *Class. Rev.*, XXXVI: 2.

(33) See H. R. Fairclough, "Horace's View of the Relations Between Satire and Comedy," *Amer. Jour. Philol.*, XXXIV (1913): 183-193.

(1) μαργίτης from μαργός, silly.

(2) *Odyss.* X. 40-75.

(3) *A. P.* 79.

(4) *Epist.* I. xix. 23-25.

(5) *Odes* II, vii. 10. For Archilochus see Bergk, *Poetae Lyrici Graeci* (4th ed.; 1882), Vol. II.

(6) Bergk, *op. cit.*, II: 451.

(7) *Poetics* v. 3.

(8) Hor. *Sat.* I. iv. 1.

(9) Ath. VIII. 59; XII. 40; X. 18; XI. 91 bis.

(10) G. A. Gerhard, *Phoinix von Kolophon: Texte u. Untersuchungen* (Leipzig, 1909).

(11) E.g., I shall not here attempt to assess the relative influence upon Horace of the Peripatetic Ariston of Ceos and of the Stoic Ariston of Chios. Several main streams of influence are summarized in Emil Englmaier's dissertation, "Was ist in des Horaz Satiren und Episteln auf griechischen Einfluss zurückzuführen?" (Nuremberg, 1913).

(12) *Epist.* II. ii. 59-60.

(13) A recent study of the Cynic diatribe is given in Terzaghi's *Per la storia della satira* (Turin, 1932), pp. 7-51.

(14) O. Hense, *Teletis Reliquiae* (Tübingen, 1909).

(15) R. Heinze, *De Horatio Bionis imitatore* (Bonn, 1889).

(16) See J. Geffcken, *Studien zur griechischen Satire*, in *Neue Jahrbücher für das klassische Altertum*, 1911, pp. 393-411, 469-493; also the two final chapters in Gerhard's *Phoinix von Kolophon*, which survey the choliambic poetry and the gnomic poetry of the Hellenistic age.

(17) παίγνια σπουδῇ λεληθυίᾳ μεμιγμένα, Diog. Laert. VI. iii. 83.

(18) *De Consolatione Philosophiae* II. metrum i.

(19) *Anthol. Palat.* VII. 472.

(20) Line 7. καὶ MS: κᾱτ᾽ Kock: ἀλλ᾽ *Meineke.* αὐτῶν MS: αὐτοῖς *Kock:* χρόνος MS: χρόνον *Grotius:* χρόνῳ *Schmidt.*

(21) Geffcken, *op. cit.*

(22) Diog. Laert. IV. vii. 49. Diogenes gives a chapter, IV. vii, to Bion.

(23) R. Helm, *Lucian und Menippus* (Leipzig, 1906).

(24) Lucian *Necyomanteia* 16.

(25) The idea of a πομπή is suggested in Teles-Bion (Hense, p. 15), ἀπαλλάττεσθαι ὥσπερ ἐκ πανηγύρεως. Bion owed it to Comedy (see Geffcken's note, *Studien z. griech. Sat.*, p. 474).

(26) *Anthol. Palat.* VI. 293.

(27) *Grammat. Lat.*, Keil, I: 485, 30, *satira dicitur carmen apud Romanos nunc quidem maledicum et ad carpenda hominum vitia archaeae comoediae compositum... et olim carmen quod ex variis poematibus constabat satira vocabatur....*

(28) Nonius 88, 5-7 (see Varro's ὄνος λύρας, 356 in Buecheler's ed. of the *Menippeae*)
Pacvi discipulus dicor, porro is fuit Enni,
Ennius Musarum, Pompilius clueor.

(29) For a recent collection of the fragments see E. H. Warmington's *Remains of Old Latin*, I (Loeb, 1935): 382 sqq.

(30) *Inst. Or.* IX. ii. 36.

(31) *Noct. Att.* XVIII. ii. 7.

(32) *Noct. Att.* VII. ix. 1.

(33) Marx, *Lucilius*, I. *Proleg.* xiv. He also suggested that Lucilius used the title *sermones per saturam*.

(34) *Phorm.* II. ii. 25. (*Donati Commentum*, ed. Wessner, p. 432.)

(35) Nonius, 66, 18, cites from Ennius ("Satyrarum, Lib. III")
testes sunt lati campi quos gerit Africa terra politos.

(36) L. Müller, *Q. Ennius: eine Einleitung in das Studium der römischen Poesie* (St. Petersburg, 1884), p. 107.

(37) Gellius, *Noct. Att.* II. xxix. O. Ribbeck, in *Rh. Mus.* X. (1856), pp. 290 sqq., attempted to restore the verse of the whole fable.

(38) *Grammat. Lat.*, Keil, IV: 401 and 565.

(39) Gellius, *Noct. Att.* XVII. xvii. 1.

(40) A. Y. Campbell, *Horace: A New Interpretation* (London, 1924), p. 149.

(41) *Sat.* II. ii. 4, *discite non inter lances mensasque nitentes* etc.

(42) *Sat.* II. iv. 11.

(43) In addition to the Ennian hexameter, Lucilius was possibly influenced by the example of the popular Greek hexameters in Hellenistic times and by the use of the hexameter by Timon of Phlius in his Σίλλοι to paraody Homer.

(1) Hor. *Sat.* II. i. 30-34.

(2) Hor. *Sat.* I. iv. 9-13; x. 1-3.

(3) *Inst. Or.* X. i. 93.

(4) *Dial. de Or.* xxiii.

(5) See J.Wight Duff, *A Literary History of Rome to the Close of the Golden Age* (1909), p. 234; and by the same author, Chap. XIII in *Cambridge Ancient History*, VIII: 417.

(6) Asconius on Cic. *In Pison.*, p. 12, 9; cf. Marx, *C. Lucil. Carm. Reliq.*, Proleg., p. xxiv.

(7) Cic. *De Orat.* II. 37.

(8) *De Amic.* xix. 69.

(9) Mrs. R. M. Brown, in *A Study of the Scipionic Circle* (University of Iowa, 1934), has endeavored to extend it backward and forward in time so as to range from Africanus Maior to Q. Lutatius Catulus. The literary coterie around the latter has been sketched separately by R. Büttner, *Porcius Licinus u. der litterarische Kreis des Q. Lutatius Catulus* (Leipzig,1893).

(10) Hor. *Sat.* II. i. 70.

(11) R.Reitzenstein, *Scipio Aemilianus und die stoische Rhetorik* (Strassburg, 1901), and *Werden und Wesen der Humanität im Altertum* (Strassb. Festschr., 1907); E. V. Arnold, *Roman Stoicism* (Cambridge, 1911); Pauly-Wissowa, *Realencycl.*, Suppl., Bd. V (1931), art. *Humanitas* by I. Heinemann, esp. sec. 6 on its implications in the republican period. See also G. C.Fiske,*Lucilius and Horace*(Madison, Wis., 1920), Chap. II.

(12) Cic. *De Officiis* I. 50. sqq.

(13) Max Pohlenz, *Antikes Führertum: Cicero De Officiis u. das Lebensideal*

des Panaitios (Leipzig, 1934). Lotte Labowsky, *Die Ethik des Panaitios* (Leipzig, 1934).

(14) *De Off.* I. 101-104.

(15) *De Off.* I. 134.

(16) Hor. *Sat.* I. iv. 1 sqq.; II. i. 67-69.

(17) Hor. *Sat.* I. x. 9 sqq.

(18) F. Marx, *C. Lucilii Carminum Reliquiae* (2 vols.; Leipzig, 1904-1905); C. Cichorius, *Untersuchungen zu Lucilius* (Berlin, 1908), and *Römische Studien* (Berlin, 1922); W. Schmitt, *Satiren Fragmente des Luc. aus den Büchern* XXVI–XXX (Munich, 1914); G. C. Fiske, *Lucilius and Horace* (Madison, Wis., 1920); N. Terzaghi, *C. Lucilii Saturarum Reliquae* (Florence,1934); *idem, Lucilio* (Turin, 1934); Kappelmacher's art. "Lucilius," Pauly-Wissowa, *Realencycl.* (1927).

(19) For a reconstruction of the argument see Fiske, *Lucilius and Horace*, p. 246.

(20) *Sat.* I. iii. 124-125.

(21) See W. Süss, *Hermes*, Bd. LXII, Hft. 3 (1927).

(22) Persius *Sat.* I. 114, *secuit Lucilius urbem*.

(23) See 1138 *Cornelius Publius noster Scipiadas;* cf. 394.

(24) *Sat.* II. i. 30 sqq.

(25) *Untersuchungen zu Lucilius*, pp. 303-315.

(26) E.g., of *hoc quidam non belle*, Hor. *Sat.* I. iv. 136, Fiske remarks that Horace apparently uses the word *belle* in recollection of the Lucilian fragment 805, . . . *bellum si hoc bellum putas*. I cannot believe that Horace needed to borrow a simple colloquial word like *belle*.

(27) Pt. I, canto i. 51-52.

(28) Cicero, *Brutus* xxxv (131), calls Albucius *paene Graecus*, informing us that at Athens "he had come out a perfect Epicurean." We owe the preservation of Lucilius' lines on the encounter to Cic. *De Fin.* I. iii. 9.

(29) Fragment 836 translates Aristophanes *Wasps*, 184. The fragments of Bk. XXIX belong to a scene usual in the New Comedy—the excluded lover; and in particular his iambics at times recall the New Comedy. One of several instances of the influence of Latin Comedy upon Lucilius is his borrowing fragment 736 from Plautus' *Mercator* 397.

(30) Words drawn from the common speech are registered in Marx's edition under "castrensis sermo."

(31) Ausonius *Epist.* v. 37-38 following his line *Villa Lucani-mox potieris -aco*, which may rank with the line apocryphally ascribed to Ennius (unless it is from his *saturae*), *Massili-portabant iuvenes ad litora -tanas.*

(32) See 198, 234, 1340 in Marx's edition.

(33) E. Norden, *Die röm. Lit.*, 100, 4.

(34) F. Marx, *op. cit.*, pp. lxxviii sqq.

(35) Th. Birt, *Zwei polit. Satiren des alten Roms* (Marburg, 1888).

(36) See Terzaghi, *Lucilio*, p. 427, "comunque sia, i defetti formali sono di gran lunga minori ed inferiori rispetto ai pregi intrinseci."

(37) *Epist.* I. iii. 15-20.

(38) See Hor. *Sat.* I. v. 82-85. Cf. Dousa's restoration of Porphyrion's quotation on *Sat.* I. vi. 22, and Lucilius 1248.

(39) E.g., Naevius and Nomentanus, *Sat.* I. i. 101-102.

(40) Cf. also *Bruttates bilingues Ennius dixit quod Bruttii et Osce et Graece loqui soliti sunt*, Paul. ex Fest. p. 35 Müll. (*Ann.* 488 Vahlen).

(41) *A.P.* 431-433; Lucilius 954 (Marx).

(42) Lucilius 1368 (Marx) = Varro *Menipp.* 417 (Buecheler): Luc. 874 = 509 Varro.

(43) See Fiske, *Lucilius and Horace*, Chap. III.

(44) *Sat.* II. i. 34.

(45) *Sat.* I. x. 48, *inventore minor;* cf. II. i. 62-63, *cum est Lucilius ausus primus in hunc operis componere carmina morem.*

(46) *Inst. Or.* X. i. 94.

(47) *Sat.* I. iv. 1-13, 56-62; x. 1-5, 20-39, 46-71; II. i. 16-17, 28-34, 62-77.

(1) *Epist.* II. i. 18-49, 115-138.

(2) *Ibid.* 189-207.

(3) *A. P.* 453 sqq.

(4) *Epist.* II. i. 250. See G. L. Hendrickson, "Are the Letters of Horace Satires?" *Am. Jour. Philol.,* XVIII (1897): 313-324.

(5) Jefferson Elmore, "A New Dating of Horace's *De Arte Poetica,*" *Class. Philol.,* XXX (1935): 1-9.

(6) C. Jensen, *Neoptolemos und Horaz* (Berlin, 1919) and *Philodemos über die Gedichte, fünftes Buch* (Berlin, 1923); O. Immisch, *Horazens Epistel über die Dichtkunst* (Leipzig, 1932).

(7) *Sat.* I. v. 51-70.

(8) It is translated as a dramatic sketch in J. Wight Duff's *A Literary History of Rome to the Close of the Golden Age,* chapter on Horace.

(9) *Sat.* I. iv. 39 sqq.

(10) *Epist.* I. ii.

(11) *Epist.* I. vi.

(12) *Sat.* II. i. 62-79.

(13) *Sat.* II. iv. 11-87.

(14) *Sat.* II. iv. 93-95; Lucr. *De Rer. Nat.* I. 927-928.

(15) The employment of proper names in the *Satires* is discussed by A. Cartault, *Etude sur les satires d'Horace* (1899), Chap. VII.

(16) *Epist.* I. i. 59.

(17) *Ibid.* 106 sqq.

(18) Some of Florus' satires, we are told by Porphyrion, were drawn from Ennius, Lucilius, and Varro.

(19) *Od.* II. vi.

(20) Martial X. xx (xix).

(21) *Epist.* I. vii. 25-28.

(22) *Epist.* I. xx. 20-28. Lollius was consul in 21 B.C. The other consulship, originally arranged for Augustus, was eventually filled by Lepidus' appointment. The variant reading for *dixit* is *duxit.*

(23) See J. Wight Duff and A. M. Duff, *Minor Latin Poets* (Loeb, 1934).

(24) *Sat.* I. iii. 99-124.

(25) *Sat.* II. ii. 135-136.

(26) *Sat.* II. iii and vii.

(27) *Sat.* II. vii. 83-88.

(28) *Od.* I. ix and xi.

(29) *Od.* I. xviii.

(30) *Od.* III. xxix. 49-56.

(31) *Od.* III. xxiii.

(32) *Od.* IV. xii. 28.

(33) *Sat.* I. i. 106.

(34) *Od.* II. x. 5-8.

(35) *Od.* III. v. 13-56; *ibid.* iii. 1-8.

(36) *Od.* II. i. 23-24.

(37) *Epist.* I. vi. 37.

(38) It is quoted in Stobaeus:

τίς δὲ βίος, τί δὲ τερπνόν, ἄτερ
χρυσέης Ἀφροδίτης; τεθναίην
ὅτε μοι μηκέτι ταῦτα μέλοι.

(1) Hor. *Sat.* I. x. 46, *experto frustra Varrone Atacino*.

(2) F. Ritschl (*Opusc.*, Bd. 3) computed Varro's total output at six hundred and twenty volumes.

(3) Text: *Varronis Menippeae*, with Petronius and *Apocolocyntosis*, F. Buecheler (Berlin, 1904); 5th ed., Buecheler-Heraeus (1912).

Studies: G. Boissier, *Etude sur la vie et les ouvrages de Varron* (Paris, 1861); Plessis-Lejay, *La Ménippée de Varron* (Paris, 1911); L. Riccomagno, *Studio sulle Satire Menippee di M. T. Varrone* (1931). Cf. J. Wight Duff, *A Literary History of Rome to the Close of the Golden Age* (1909), pp. 334 sqq.; C. Cichorius, *Röm. Studien* (Leipzig, 1922), pp. 189 sqq.; E. Norden, *Röm. Lit.* (Leipzig, 1933).

For sketches reconstructing fragments of several satires see Mommsen, *Rom. Hist.*, Eng. trans., IV: 596 sqq.; W. W. Merry, *Fragments of Roman Poetry* (Oxford, 1891), pp. 196 sqq.; E. T. Merrill, *Fragments of Roman Satire* (New York, 1897).

For a conspectus of the literature of reconstruction and interpretation of the fragments see Schanz-Hosius, *Röm. Literaturgesch.*, 4th ed. (1927), I: 560.

(4) *Ad Att.* XIII. 25. 3.

(5) Buecheler, fr. 404.

(6) *Noct. Att.* XIII. xxix.

(8) Buecheler, fr. 516.

(9) Buecheler, fr. 122.

(10) Cic. *Acad. Post.* I. ii. 8, *In illis ve-*

teribus nostris quae Menippum imitati, non interpretati, quadam hilaritate conspersimus, multa admixta ex intima philosophia, multa dicta dialectice....

(11) Buecheler, fr. 556.

(12) Schanz-Hosius, *op. cit.*, p. 560.

(13) Buecheler, fr. 53, 398, 417.

(14) Buecheler, fr. 59, 522.

(15) E. Norden, *op. cit.*, 24.

(16) For an English verse translation see J. Wight Duff, *op. cit.*, p. 337.

(17) Buecheler, fr. 89.

(18) Buecheler, fr. 111.

(19) E.g., Stahr, *Agrippina*, Append. (Berlin, 1867); Birt, *De Sen. Apoc. et Apoth. lucubratio* (Marburg, 1888), thinks Seneca wrote the extant political satire but also a lost philosophical *Apocolocyntosis*. Hartman, *Mnemos.*, n. s., XLIV (1916), believes the "Pumpkinification" to have been distinct from the existing skit.

(20) Dio lx. 35.

(21) Petron. 39; Juv. XIV. 58; Apul. *Met.* I. xv. H. Wagenvoort, *Mnemos.*, n. s., LXII (1934): 4-27, rejects the current view of ἀποκολοκύντωσις as transformation into a pumpkin or fool for the reason that Claudius was already a booby. On the analogy of the punishment ἀποραφανίδωσις, he explains it as Seneca's revenge on Claudius.

(22) This is Hirschfeld's opinion (*Kl. Schriften*, 1913) and it is accepted by Bickel in "Der Schluss d. Apocol.," *Philol.*, LXXVII (1921). Cf. Suet. *Claud.* 45.

(23) F. Buecheler (with Petronius, etc.), 4th ed. (Berlin, 1904); 5th ed., Buecheler-Heraeus (1922); A. P. Ball (text, trans., comm.; New York, 1902); W. H. D. Rouse *in* Loeb ed. (with Petronius) (London and New York, 1913); O. Weinreich, *Senecas Apocol. . . . Einführung, Analyse, Untersuchung* (Berlin, 1923). Cf. J. Wight Duff, *A Literary History of Rome in the Silver Age* (1927); pp. 237-246; A. Momigliano, *Claudius: The Emperor and His Achievement* . . . (trans. by W. D. Hogarth; Oxford, 1934), Chap. IV, pp. 74-79.

(24) The couplet is borrowed from J. Wight Duff, *A Literary History of Rome in the Silver Age*, p. 238.

(25) Suet. *Cal.* 22.

(26) *Claudius*, Eng. trans., p. 75.

(27) Tac. *Ann.* XV. 49; schol. ad Juv. IV. 106; Suet. *Dom.* i.

(28) To Petronius' miscellany Buecheler gives the title *saturae*. If that was Petronius' own title, he used it in Varro's sense. Marx, *Lucilius*, p. x, thinks the word *satyricus* did not come into use before the third century A.D.—unless we accept the title of Petronius' MSS as going back to the author's time.

(29) *Petronii Saturae*, F. Buecheler: vi ed. auctam curavit G. Heraeus (Berlin, 1922); text, with Eng. trans., M. Heseltine (Loeb) (London and New York, 1913); *Cena Trimalchionis* (Germ. trans. and notes), L. Friedlaender, 2d ed. (1906); *Cena* (with *Apocolocyntosis*) ed. W. B. Sedgwick (Oxford, 1925).
Consult J. Wight Duff, *A Literary History of Rome in the Silver*

Age (London, 1927), pp. 169 sqq.; C. Beck, *The Age of Petronius* (Cambridge, Mass., 1856); G. Boissier, "Un Roman de mœurs sous Néron," in *L'Opposition sous les Césars* (Paris, 1875); S. Dill, *Roman Society from Nero to M. Aurelius* (London, 1904); C. Whibley, *Studies in Frankness* (London, 1926), pp. 29-48; H. Stubbe, "Die Verseinlagen im Petron," *Philologus*, Suppl., Bd. XXV, Hft. 2 (1933); E. H. Haight, *Essays on Ancient Fiction*; esp. Chap. III, "Satire and the Latin Novel" (New York, 1936).
On language: Guericke, *De linguae vulgaris reliquiis apud Petronium et in inscriptionibus parietariis Pompeianis* (diss.; Königsberg, 1875); Grandgent, *An Introduction to Vulgar Latin* (1907); W. Suess, *De eo quem dicunt inesse Trimalchionis cenae sermone vulgari* (Dorpat, 1926).

(30) Tac. *Ann.* XVI. 18-19.

(31) Servius *ad Aen.* III. 57; cf. Sidon. Apollinar. xxiii. 155-157.

(32) ἐγκόλπιος = "in or on the bosom"; ἄσκυλτος = "unhurt," "scatheless"; γείτων = "neighbor."

(33) Petron. *Sat.* 48.

(34) *Ibid.* 41.

(35) *Ibid.* 42.

(36) *Ibid.* 43.

(37) *Ibid.* 44.

(38) *Ibid.* 46.

(39) See A. H. Salonius, "Die Griechen und das Griechische in Petrons *Cena Trimalchionis*," (Helsingfors, Soc. Scient. Fennica, 1927).

(40) *Satyr.* 61-62; 63.

(41) *Ibid.* 111-112.

(42) E.g., *Satyr.* 119-124, a rewriting of part of Lucan in two hundred and ninety-five hexameters (see *infra*); iambics on the capture of Troy (based on *Aeneid* II), 89; hendecasyllables, 15, 93; elegiacs, 18, 34. Other poems ascribed to Petronius include his very beautiful sonnet-like piece in elegiac lines on a sleepless lover (*lecto compositus vix prima silentia noctis* . . .): see J.Wight Duff, *op. cit.*, 193-195.

(43) J. Geffcken, "Studien zur griech. Sat.," *Neue Jahrb.f.d.klass.Altert.* (1911), p. 485, refers to Rohde, *Der griech. Roman.*, 2d ed., p. 267, Hirzel, *Der Dialog.*, II: 37, and W. Schmid, *Neue Jahrb.* (1904), XIII: 476, in support of the view that regards Petronius' romance as an extended Menippean Satire. Cf.

Rosenblüth, *Beiträge zur Quellenkunde von Petrons Satiren* (Berlin, 1909).

(44) See *Satyr.* 111-112, and for Milesian tales cf. Norden, *Die antike Kunstprosa*, II. 602, 604 n.; Rohde, *op. cit.*, and *Kl. Schr.* (1901) II. 25 sqq.; Lucas, "Zu den Milesiaca des Aristides," *Philologus*, LXI (1907); 16 sqq.

(45) Révay's article, "Horaz und Petron," *Class. Phil.*, XVII (1922): 202, illustrates the influence of Hor. *Sat.* II. 8 on Trimalchio's banquet.

(46) *Satyr.* 116, *aut captantur aut captant.*

(47) *Ibid.* 1-5.

(48) *Ibid.* 118.

(49) *Ibid.* 119-124.

(50) *Ibid.* 120.

(1) Phaedrus: L. Havet, *Phaedri Augusti liberti fabulae Aesopiae* (1895) and *Phèdre* (1896; 14th ed., 1923); J. Gow, in Postgate's *Corpus Poetarum Latinorum*, II (London, 1905); F. Ramorino, *Le Favole di Fedro* (5th ed.; Torino, 1915); A. Brenot, *Phèdre* (texte et traduction; Paris, 1924). Cf. L. Hervieux, *Les fabulistes latins jusqu'à la fin du moyen-âge* (2d ed.; 5 vols., 1893 sqq.); H. Vandaele, *Qua mente Phaeder fabellas scripserit* (thesis; Paris, 1897); J. Wight Duff, *A Literary History of Rome in the Silver Age* (London, 1927), pp. 133-154; N. Terzaghi, *Per la storia della satira* (Torino, 1932), pp. 59-90.

(2) Hor. *Sat.* I. i. 32-38.

(3) *Proverbs*, vi. 6-9.

(4) III. *Epil. 33-34.*

(5) IV. vii. For Simonides see IV. xxii (xxiii) and xxv (xxvi). III. prol. 27-28 quotes Virgil.

(6) Terzaghi, *Per la storia della satira*, pp. 69-70.

(7) II. *Epil.* 8-9.

(8) I. *prol.* 1-7. The translation here, and in a few other passages, is borrowed from J. Wight Duff's *Literary History of Rome in the Silver Age*, p. 138.

(9) We may guess that he was born about 15 B.C.

(10) V. x. 9-10.

(11) Terzaghi, *op. cit.*, p. 62.

(12) Avianus, the other fabulist of Rome, in his dedicatory letter mentions both Phaedrus and Babrius as predecessors; but he owes more to the Greek fables of Babrius: see *Minor Latin Poets*, ed. and trans. by J. Wight Duff and A. M. Duff (London and Cambridge, Mass., 1934), pp. 669-749.

(13) Mart. III. xx. 5. Friedländer prefers to think an obscure writer of mimes may be meant. Thiele, *Philol.*, LXX (1911) (N. F., Bd. XXIV): 539 sqq., substitutes *logos* (=*apologos*) for *iocos*, and takes *improbi* to imply audacious political allusions by Phaedrus.

(14) II. *prol.* 2-3.

(15) II. *prol.* 8-11.

(16) III. *prol.* 33-37. The whole passage 33-63 is transferred by Havet from III. *prol.* to II. *prol.*

(17) III. *prol.* 49-51.

(18) V. vii.

(19) II. v.

(20) I. iii; iv; xvii; xxiii; xxv.

(21) IV. xvii. 9-10.

(22) I. x. 9-10.

(23) III. 13.

(24) I. xiv. 14-16, where the Latin has the advantage of the contrast between *capita* and *pedes*.

(25) IV. xx.

(26) IV. xviii.

(27) V. v.

(28) That is, his iambic line is not that of Catullus or Horace: Phaedrus admits spondees in the second and the fourth feet.

(29) V. iii. 5.

(30) Text: I. Casaubon (Paris, 1605); cum schol.,O. Jahn (Leipzig, 1843); 3d ed. (with Juvenal), Buecheler (1893); 4th ed., Leo (1910); 5th ed., 1932; with trans. and comm., Conington, ed. Nettleship (Oxford, 1872); Gildersleeve (New York, 1875); étude et trad. franc., Rousse (Paris, 1884); (with Juvenal) Owen (Oxford, 1902); in *Corp. Poet. Lat.*, Summers (London, 1905); Santi Consoli (Rome, 1911); Van Wageningen (Groningen, 1911); (with Juvenal, Eng. trans.) G. G. Ramsay (Loeb) (London, 1918); Villeneuve (Paris, 1918); Ramorino (Turin, 1920); A. Cartault (texte et trad. franc.) (Paris, 1920; 2d ed., 1929).

Consult: Morgan, *A Bibliography of P.* (Cambridge, Mass., 1893); Martha, "Un Poète Stoicien," in *Les Moralistes sous l'empire rom.* (1865); Villeneuve, *Essai sur Perse* (Paris, 1918), bibliog.; J. Wight Duff, *A Literary History of Rome in the Silver Age* (London, 1927), pp. 279-295.

Verse translations: Dryden (1693); W. Gifford, reprinted with his trans. of Juvenal in Bohn's Classical Library (London, 1877); J. Tate (Oxford, 1930).

(31) The main facts of Persius' life are given in a *Vita* taken from a Commentary by Valerius Probus in the latter half of the first century.

(32) Th. Werther's *De Persio Horatii Imitatore* (Halle, 1883), closes with a summary of defects in Persius' style. Useful tables of parallels with Horace, Catullus, Virgil, and Ovid are given in Van Wageningen's edition.

(33) *Satyr.* 4. Cf. G. C. Fiske, "Lucilius and Persius," *Trans. Amer. Phil. Assoc.*, XL (1909): 121-150.

(34) *Prol.* 3; *Sat.* VI. 10-11.

(35) *Sat.* I. 76-78.

(36) *Sat.* VI. 3-4.

(37) For the pre-Augustan taste at Nero's court, e.g., for Catullus in preference to Virgil, see B. L. Gildersleeve's Persius, Introd., p. xxiv.

(38) *Inst. Or.* X. i. 94.

(39) Villeneuve, *Essai sur Perse*, p. 179.

(40) Tac. *Hist.* III. 81: cf. *Ann.* XIV. 59, XV. 71.

(41) III. 66 sqq. (*discite, o miseri . . .*); V. 66 (*cras hoc fiet . . .*); V. 73 sqq.

(42) A. Cartault, *Revue de Philologie*, XLV (1921): 63, thinks it an unfinished early poem, with the first seven lines put in the mouth of an anonymous poet and the last seven giving Persius' answer.

(43) A. Cartault, *Revue de Philologie*, XLV. (1921): 66 sqq., thinks that probably it was composed when Persius was eighteen years old, in A.D. 52.

(44) Sen. *Epist.* 114.

(45) A. Cartault, *Revue de Philologie*, XLV (1921): 66 sqq., thinks the four lines may be quoted from one of Nero's early compositions.

(46) Catull. xxii. 21; Hor. *Sat.* II. 3. 299; Phaedrus, IV. x.

(47) Hor. *Sat.* II. vii.

(48) Quint. *Inst. Or.* VIII. ii. 18.

(49) The influence of the *sermo popularis* is more marked in Persius than in Horace, and is a reversion to Lucilian style, as is his use of the first personal pronoun.

(50) Elzevir ed. (Leyden, 1629), p. 227.

(1) Friedländer (introd., German comm.; 2 vols.; Leipzig, 1886); Lindsay (Oxford, 1902); J. D. Duff, *in* Postgate's *Corp. Poet. Lat.* (London, 1905); Ker (with Eng. prose trans., Loeb ser.; 2 vols.; London and New York, 1919-1920); Heraeus (Leipzig, 1925).

Selections: Stephenson (4th ed.; London, 1899); Bridge and Lake (Oxford, 1908).

Other Works: Friedländer, *Darstellungen aus der Sittengeschichte Roms* (9th ed.; Wissowa, Leipzig, 1919-1921); Eng. trans. from 7th German ed. (London, 1908-1913). K. Flower Smith, *M. the Epigrammatist and Other Essays* (Baltimore, 1920); J. Wight Duff, *A Literary History of Rome in the Silver Age* (London, 1927), pp. 498-529; Schanz-Hosius, *Geschichte der römischen Literatur in der Zeit der Monarchie bis auf Hadrian* (München, 1935), pp. 546-560.

On Martial's models: Paukstadt, *De Martiale Catulli imitatore* (diss.; Halle, 1876); Zingerle, *Mart. Ovidstudien* (Innsbruck, 1877); Schulze, *Mart. Catullstudien, Fleck. Jahrb.*, 137 (1887); Wagner, *De Martiale poetarum Augusteae aetatis imitatore* (Königsberg, 1880); Pertsch, *De Valerio Martiale Graecorum poetarum imitatore* (diss.; Berlin, 1911).

(2) XII. 94, 7, *audemus saturas: Lucilius esse laboras.*

(3) See Reitzenstein, art. "Epigramm," *in* Pauly-Wissowa, *Realencyclopaedie* (Stuttgart, 1907).

(4) See Geffcken, *Studien zur griechischen Satire* (1911).

(5) E.g., *Anth. Pal.* XI. 414, the suspension of ποδάγρα to the close.

(6) *Anth. Pal.* IX. 572, 8.

(7) *Anth. Pal.* XI. 257.

(8) Mart. VI. 53.

(9) V. 5. 6, *qua Pedo qua Marsus quaque Catullus erit.*

(10) Baehrens, *Fragmenta Poetarum Romanorum* (1886), pp. 346, 351, 361.

(11) *Epist. ex. Ponto* IV. 10.

(12) See Catull. 67, 70, 77, 84, 93.

(13) Catull. 6, 12, 14, 15, 16, 23, 36, 57.

(14) Catull. 22, 39.

(15) Catull. 52, 29.

(16) For the poems ascribed to Petronius see Baehrens, *P. L. M.*, IV: 88-110; Petronius (Loeb ed.), pp. 340-363.

(17) Baehrens, *P. L. M.*, IV, no. 78.

(18) Baehrens, *P. L. M.*, IV, no. 86.

(19) *Ibid.*, no. 81, ll. 12-14. For *i nunc* see Hor. *Epist.* I. vi. 17.

(20) Mart. VI. 65. 4-6.

(21) IX. 73, 7-8.

(22) VII. 22: cf. 21 and 23.

(23) IV. 55, 8-11.

(24) III. 14.

(25) I. 113.

(26) V. 34; I. 88.

(27) IV. 44. 4; IX. 61.11-14.

(28) I. 117. 7, *et scalis habito tribus sed altis.*

(29) XI. 24; cf. VII. 39.

(30) XI. 3. 7-10.

(31) X. 72.

(32) XII. 18.

(33) Plin. *Epist.* III. 21.

(34) Mart. IV. 49. 1-2.

(35) V. 16. 1-4.

(36) B. H. Kennedy, in his *Between Whiles* (1877), pp. 60-61, translates Klopstock's lines into Latin elegiacs:

Nunc Epigramma ferit figentis
more sagittae;
nunc acie, gladii more secan-
tis agit:
nunc, ut apud Graecos, quo lu-
mine picta tabella
vel iubar, irradiat nec tamen
urit idem.

(37) VIII. 3. 19-20.
(38) I. 1. 2-3; XI. 3, 5.
(39) X. 9.
(40) X. 70.
(41) I. 20.
(42) IV. 66.
(43) V. 81.
(44) I. 15.
(45) V. 58. 7-8.
(46) V. 20. 11-14.
(47) IV. 64.
(48) I. 33; III. 43; IV. 53.
(49) Mart. I. 30; Juv. X. 221.
(50) Mart. IX. 96.
(51) Juv. III. 212-222.
(52) Mart. V. 47.
(53) VII. 20; IX. 10. 4.
(54) E.g., V. 20.
(55) XI. 24.
(56) VII. 39.
(57) X. 8.
(58) I. 10.
(59) IV. 41: cf. Juv. I. 11-12.
(60) Plin. *Ep.* III. 16, 6.
(61) Mart. I. 13.
(62) II. 66; cf. Juv. VI. 486 sqq.
(63) IV. 24: cf. Juv. I. 69-72.
(64) Mart. V. 68.
(65) *Anth. Pal.* XI. 68 and 310.
(66) Mart. I. 71.
(67) X. 4.
(68) V. 53.
(69) I. 76, 13.
(70) VIII, 69.
(71) I. 4, 8.
(72) V. 15.
(73) VII. 85.
(74) VI. 61, 10.

(1) *Juvenal: Select Bibliography.* Editions. Heinrich (with scholia vetera) (2 vols.; Bonn, 1839): Jahn-Buecheler-Leo, 4th ed. (Berlin, 1910), 5th ed. (1932); J. E. B. Mayor (XIII satires), 4th ed. (2 vols.; London, 1889); Friedländer (2 vols.; Leipzig, 1895); E. G. Hardy (XIII Satires), 2d ed. (London, 1891); J. D. Duff (omitting II and IX) (Cambridge, 1898, 1900 and 1914); H. L. Wilson (New York, 1903); Housman (2d ed., Cambridge, 1931); and in *Corp. Poet. Lat.* (London, 1905).

Translations: Dryden and others (w. Persius) (London, 1693); Gifford (London, 1802). In prose, S. G. Owen (London, 1903); G. G. Ramsay (w. Persius, Loeb ed.) (London, 1918).

Studies: Ribbeck, *Der echte und der unechte Juvenal* (Berlin, 1865); Boissier, *L'opposition sous les Césars* (Paris, 1875); Dürr, *Das Leben Juv.* (Ulm, 1888); Nettleship, *Life and Poems of Juv.*, in *Lects. and Essays*, ser. 2 (Oxford, 1895); Martha, *Les moralistes sous l'empire romain*, 8th ed. (1907); J. Wight Duff, *A Literary History of Rome in the Silver Age* (London, 1927); Schanz-Hosius, *Geschichte der röm. Lit.*, Teil 2, 4th ed. (München, 1935).

On Style: Wilcke, *Disp. quid elocutio Juvenalis a Persiana differat* (Stendal, 1869); Schwartz, *De Juv. Horatii imitatore* (Halle, 1882); Gehlen, *De Juv. Vergili imitatore* (Göttingen, 1886); Eskuche, *Juvenals Versbau*, offprint

from Friedländer's ed. (Leipzig 1895); Wilson, "Literary Influence of Martial Upon Juvenal," *Amer. Jour. Philol.* (1898); De Decker, *Juvenalis Declamans (étude sur la rhétorique déclamatoire dans les satires de Juvénal)* (Gand, 1913): cf. Cucheval, *Histoire de l'éloquence rom. depuis la mort de Cicéron jusqu'à Hadrien* (Paris, 1893): Boissier, *Les écoles de déclamation à Rome*, in his *Tacite*, 2d ed. (Paris, 1904); Bornecque, *Les déclamations et les déclamateurs d'après Sénèque le père* (Lille, 1902); I. G. Scott, *The Grand Style in the Satires of Juvenal* (Northampton, Mass.), 1927.

(2) Mart. VII. 24 and 91; XII. 18.

(3) Juv. VII. 124-125 *et melius nos egimus:* see Merchant, *Amer. Jour. Philol.*, XXII (1901): 51 sqq.

(4) Juv. X. 289-345: see O. Kiefer, *Kulturgeschichte Roms* (Berlin, 1933), p. 286.

(5) J. Wight Duff, *A Literary History of Rome in the Silver Age*, pp. 599-604.

(6) *tuo . . . Aquino, Sat.* III. 319. See *C. I. L.* X. 5382 = Dessau, *Insc. Lat. Sel.*, I. 2926.

(7) Our extant textual tradition probably rests on an edition in the second half of the fourth century. Leo, "Doppelfassungen bei Juvenal," *Hermes*, XLIV (1909): 600 sqq., argued for two editions, one issued by the author, the other (with alterations) being posthumous. If commentators had access to both, there was a possibility of interpolation.

(8) XIII. 17; XV. 27, *nuper consule Iunco.*

(9) XI. 65, 190.

(10) Juv. I. 101 sqq.

(11) VI. 440-442.

(12) III. 198 sqq.

(13) IV. 153-154; 37-38.

(14) Mart. I. 20.

(15) Juv. V. 112.

(16) *ibid.* 156-158; 170-171.

(17) VIII. 83-84.

(18) VI. 346-366. The translation is in part rewritten from that in my volume on the "Silver Age," p. 618.

(19) XI. 203-204.

(20) XIII. 189 sqq.

(21) I. 93; IV. 117.

(22) II. 143 sqq., VIII. 185-192, 198 sqq.

(23) II. 149-158.

(24) Compare Persius III with Juvenal VIII.

(25) VIII. 20-21, 30.

(26) IV. 47-48.

(27) X. 81.

(28) E.g., III. 152-153, 162-167.

(29) I. 119-120.

(30) Persius V. 73-74.

(31) Juv. X. 77-78.

(32) See A. M. Duff, *Freedmen in the Early Roman Empire* (Oxford, 1928), esp. Chaps. II and IX.

(33) Juv. I, 64; III. 285-288, 261-264, 183-189.

(34) V. 54.

(35) I. 79.

(36) De Decker, *Juvenalis Declamans* (Gand, 1913), pp. 19-20, 54 sqq., opposes Schütze's theory of direct influence of the Stoic system on Juvenal: see Schütze, *Juvenalis Ethicus* (diss.; Greifswald, 1905).

(37) E.g., *Sat.* I. 30-34, 63-72.

(38) Hor. *Sat.* I. x. 46.

(39) Varro *De Re Rust.* III. ii. 17.

(40) Suet. *De Gramm.* 5.

(41) Suet. *De Gramm.* 15.

(42) Suet. *Claud.* 38, 3.

(43) Tac. *Ann.* XIV. 48; XVI. 28.

(44) Stat. *Silv.* I. iii. 102-103, *liventem satiram nigra . . . sive rubigine vibres.*

(45) Mart. XI. 10.

(46) Juv. I. 80.

(47) Plin. *Epist.* III. 15.

(48) *Sulpiciae Fabella,* ed. Unger (Halle, 1887).

(49) *Latin Satirical Writing Subsequent to Juvenal* (Lancaster, Pa., 1915).

(50) I. 381-398, 441-452: cf. attack on Stilicho, *De Reditu,* II. 41-60 in *Minor Latin Poets,* J. Wight Duff and A. M. Duff (Loeb) (London and Cambridge, Mass., 1934).

(51) *Elegantiores Praestantium Virorum Satyrae* (2 vols.; Leyden, 1655).

INDEX

INDEX

Abuccius (or Albucius), L., satirist, 164

Academica, 85

Accius: *Didascalica* of, 51; hits at, by Lucilius, 52; comparison of style of, with Greek models, 57; Varro influenced by, 90; style of, 116

Aesop: traditional father of prose beast story, 25, 108; an adaptation by Ennius, 40; Phaedrus' belief in, as author of fables, 108; Phaedrus his Latin counterpart, 110

Afranius Quintianus, 17; verse attack of Nero upon, 96, 164

Agriculture (Res Rusticae); of Varro, 85

Albucius. *See* Abuccius

Ammianus, use of *invectiva* in, 13

Annales of Ennius, 44, 51, 52; of Tacitus, 96

Anthologia Latina, 91

Anthologia Palatina, 26, 32, 126, 127. *See* Greek Anthology

Antiochus, follower of Panaetius' system of *humanitas*, 46

Antiquitates, 85

Apocolocyntosis: its *Divine Council* goes back to Homer, Menippus, and Lucilius, 24, 37; Seneca's authorship of, 91; meaning of word, 92; a satire on deification of Claudius, 84, 92, 93 ff.; hint to write, may have come from Nero, 96

Apophoreta, 132

Apuleius: satiric intention in *Golden Ass* by, 104; realism of, 104; bizarre Latinity of, 104; style of, contrasted with that of Petronius, 104

Archilochus: satiric writings of, 24; found that rage begot verse, 24; iambic measures of, introduced into Latium, 24; invective force of, 24; self-revelation of, 25; fox stories of, 25; the iambic satirist, 28

Ardaliones, satirized, 111

Aristius Fuscus: friend of Horace, 69, 77; Acron ascribes tragedies to, 77; Porphyrion, on the other hand, ascribes comedies to, 77

Aristophanes: satire in *Birds* of, 5, 36; function of plays of, 6; effect of, on writings of Lucilius, 22, 26, 62; amusement combined with abuse of evildoers, 26; satire only a factor in plays of, 26; verbal imitations of, by Lucilius, 57

Aristotle, satirical attacks pointed out by, 23

Arria: Persius' lines on, lost, 116; Martial not blind to nobility of, 142

Ars Poetica, 3, 59, 65-66, 68

Athenaeus, quotations of choliambics of Phoenix in, 27

Attic Comedy: alleged insertion of *satura* in Livy's account of drama to match, 19-20; Horace on Lucilius' relation to, 20-22, 48, 62; various representatives of, 28

Attic Nights, 16

Augustus: settlement of Rome's difficulties under, 45; an epistle of Horace meant for entourage of, 60; contact of Horace with, 67; on presenting Horatian poetry to, at a suitable moment, 75

Aulularia, 12

Battle of the Frogs and the Mice, The, 23-24

Bible: satire in, 4; fable in, 106

Bilbilis: Martial born at, 131; an uncouth name, 131; gift of land at, to Martial, 134-135

Bion: a representative of Cynic satire, 28, 29; debt of Horace to, 28, 29, 33, 35; "jocular-earnest" diatribe of, 29; studied at Athens, 33;

Rome—*Continued*
of Horace on prosperity of, 80; hope of Seneca for a better age in, 96; testimony of Pliny to good women of, 151, 157; Juvenal held a mirror up to a degenerate, 161

Rufinus, Claudian's invective against, 165

Rutilius Namatianus: Jews disliked by, 117; couples names of Turnus and Juvenal as satirists, 165; scathing references of, to Jews and Christians, 165

Sallust, attack on, by Lenaeus, 164
Sardi Venales, 96
Satire: a recurring feature in literature, 1, 2, 3-4; two meanings of, 2; definition of, 2, 3; of sarcastic counsel, 4; expansion of old Roman conception of, 4, 12; in epigram form, 5; kinship between comedy and, 6; social outlook of, 6; vital importance of, 6; appeal made by, 7; keenness of observation necessary for, 7; Swift's definition of, 8; a literary medicine, 8, 161; function and motives of, 9-10; methods of, 10; form of, 10; close to workaday concerns, 10; a difference between contemporary and ancient, 10-11; the great English representatives of, 11-12; incidental, 12-13; *sermo* not applicable to broader modern sense of, 13; influence of Juvenal on modern, 18; Lucilius typical of Roman kind of, 18, 61; question of connection between dramatic *satura* and literary, 20; contradictory statements about ancient, 20; claimed for the Romans, 20; spirit of, is universal, 20; in Greek literature, 21, 23-38; originality of form in Lucilian, 21, 47; parody and burlesque are forms of, 23, 24; Council in

Satire—*Continued*
heaven an old motif in, 24; self-revelation a trait of, 24-25; is only a factor in comedy, 26; verse-forms used in ancient, 32; Ennius opens literary history of, in Latin, 38; in the days of the younger Scipio, 44-45; censoriousness in, 48; a kinship with prose in, 62; danger of offense in, 63; of Horace, 64 ff.; keynote and justification of, 77; Menippean, 84 ff.; of Varro, 85 ff.; of Seneca, in *Apocolocyntosis*, 91-96; of Petronius, in *Satyricon*, 96-105; of Phaedrus, 106 ff.; in fables, 106 ff.; political, 110; veiled, 110; of Persius, 114 ff.; of Martial, 131 ff.; dinner party theme for, 140-141; legacy-hunting dealt with in, 141; of Juvenal, 147 ff.; essence of, 161; classic permanence of appeal achieved by, 163; continuance after Juvenal, 165; social value of, 166. *See also* Roman satire; *satura;* Traditional themes

Satiric: element in Greek literature, 10, 23 ff., 26; varied Greek verse-forms used to carry, ideas, 32

Satirist: reformative aim of, 8, 166; a kind of doctor, 8; means employed by, 10; modern, 10-11; ancient, 11; beast story used by, 25; persistent trait of a, 37; days of the younger Scipio seemed to invite a, 44-45; Lucilius an honest, 56; highly finished style not expected in a, 57; outlook on life crucial in a, 110; must see more vice than virtue in what he attacks, 112; Martial's points of contact with a traditional, 137-138; business of the, 161; should not waste force on the superficial, 163

Satirists: English, 2-3, 11; elements in Greek tradition inherited by, of